THE MEN

WHO CHANGED

THE WORLD

By the Same Author

Nazi Luftwaffe Bomber Finishes
Nazi Luftwaffe Dope Schemes
Fighters in the Battle of Britain
Flying Bomb
Operation Thunderbolt ('Operaatio Ukonnuoli' in Finland)
1940 The Story of No. 11 Group Fighter Command
Focke Wulf Fw 190A
Messerschmitt Bf 109E
Advanced Jetliners
Flight Royal
The Aviation Enthusiast's Guide to London and the South East
Aviation Anniversaries, 1979
Sopwith Fighters in Action
The Battle of Britain
The Bristol Fighter in Action
The DH9 in Action
The Air VCs
The Encyclopedia of Air Warfare
The RFC/RNAS Handbook, 1914/1918
The DH2 in Action
German Bombers of the First World War
Nieuport Fighters in Action
British Bombers of the First World War
The Skybird Story
World War One British Propellers
Skill and Devotion (Editor)

THE MEN
WHO CHANGED
THE WORLD

The Aviation
Pioneers
1903–1914

PETER G. COOKSLEY

SUTTON PUBLISHING

First published in 2003 by
Sutton Publishing Limited · Phoenix Mill
Thrupp · Stroud · Gloucestershire · GL5 2BU

British Library Cataloguing in Publication Data
A catalogue record for this book is available from the British Library.

ISBN 0 7509 2841 7

Typeset in 12/15 pt Sabon.
Typesetting and origination by
Sutton Publishing Limited.
Printed and bound in England by
J.H. Haynes & Co. Ltd, Sparkford.

CONTENTS

. . . incontestably the Wright brothers alone resolved in its entirety the problem of human mechanical flight . . . the brothers Wilbur and Orville more than anyone else deserve the success they achieved. They changed the face of the globe.

Charles Dollfus, Former Curator, Musée de l'Air, Paris

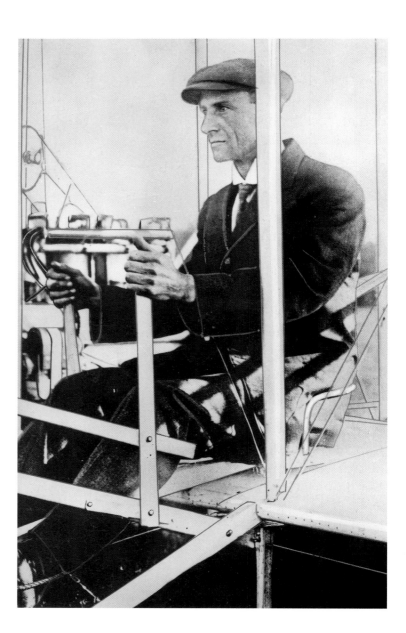

Wilbur Wright at the controls of a later Wright biplane.

ACKNOWLEDGEMENTS

Reading a book of this nature, it is all too easy to believe that the author is the only person responsible for its appearance in the bookshops. In fact, he is in a position similar to that of a television presenter, giving a human face to his subject but actually representing a large number of people through whose hands his work passes, the final product standing or falling by the standards of care, professionalism and diligence of this largely unsung group.

The same is true of the preparation, when a large number of reference works must be consulted and compared in the light of the author's knowledge, the process augmented by further research and, if possible, by interviews with those who have specialist knowledge or perhaps a personal involvement. Many of this group are the keepers of archives and records, and I would like to express grateful thanks to those performing such tasks at the Science Museum and Smithsonian Institution, and in the many public libraries where half-forgotten books were unearthed for my study; I am also grateful to such doyens of aviation history as the ever-helpful and vastly experienced Bruce Robertson, whose friendship I have had the privilege of enjoying for a very long time, and to other enthusiasts. Among these, particular mention is due to picture researcher Ann Tilbury; several members of Cross and Cockade International, the fruits of whose researches have been published in that organisation's *Journal*; Croydon Airport Society's Mike Marshall and Tom Samson; Air Historical Society of New Zealand members John Best and John Cross; Mrs Jan McGregor, daughter of the late John Garwood of that organisation; as well as Mrs Yvonne C. Bonham, Colin J. Ashford, Norman W. Cruwys, Howard Ford and Harry N.R. Wylie. All of these have pointed me in the right direction, given material help or assisted by a chance remark, often when it seemed all avenues of research had been unrewardingly explored, and I have consulted Tom Crouch's masterly book *The Bishop's Boys* for clarification of certain problematical facts.

Unfortunately, despite diligent searching, it has proved impossible to discover the identity of copyright holders of a few of the photographs used, so that apologies are tendered to them *in absentia*.

Peter G. Cooksley
London, 2003

PREFACE

I make no secret of my plans for the reason that I believe no financial profit will accrue to the inventor of the first flying machine, and that only those who are willing to give as well as to receive suggestions can hope to link their names with the honor of discovery. The problem is too great for one man alone and unaided to solve the secret.

Wilbur Wright, May 1900

To imagine a world without flight is virtually impossible since man's long-sought ability to navigate the heavens has brought him almost god-like powers of traversing space, and perhaps within the lives of our grandchildren he will conquer even time itself. But such achievements go hand in hand with offering his fellows a choice between succour or awesome destruction, so that the very wisdom of mankind is challenged.

It comes, therefore, as a surprise of some magnitude that the opening of this veritable Pandora's Box took place a mere century ago – a span negligible to an adult, inconceivable to a child. But the disbelief that greeted the young Wright brothers' success is easier to understand when viewed in context: their social background was little removed from that of the Victorian age which had dominated the known world for so long and had drawn to a close only two years before the world's first flight took place, in an obscure part of North Carolina. Those were the days when Europe held sway over the civilised world, with Britain radiating the self-confidence and enjoying the respect which is paid the United States today, but this world – removed from our own by little more than the span of the average lifetime – could not have been more different.

The United States, where the momentous first navigation of the sky had been made, was a political construct, the result of a civil war. Theodore Roosevelt, who had distinguished himself in that struggle, was later elected President only two years before the world's first successful flight – and would eventually become one of the Wright brothers' first passengers, in an America in which the Great Treks to found new communities were still a recent memory.

However, none of this is to say that the two young American citizens enjoyed any unique qualities that gave them an advantage over their European cousins. The mastery of flight might equally have been achieved by a Frenchman, a German, a Dane or an Englishman: perhaps by Horatio Philips who successfully flew a 5-hp steam-powered, tethered model in 1893; or George Holt-Thomas who hired Paulhan to give an exhibition at Brooklands in 1911; or Frank McClean who rented his flying field to the Admiralty for one shilling (5p) per annum. There were also lady pioneers such as Mrs Maurice Hewlett, who taught her son to fly in 1912, and Eleanor Trehawke Davies who had flown in her own Blériot monoplane with Hamel at the controls the year before. And there were many others, some of whose work is described in this volume. The humble realisation of this fact doubtless prompted Wilbur Wright to observe in 1903, 'Isn't it astonishing that all these secrets have been preserved for so many years, just so we could discover them', a remark demonstrating his strong religious beliefs.

But for a full understanding of the dawn of aeronautics it is necessary to view their introduction against the background of other dramatic changes that were taking place as the new century opened. Of course, many people were ignorant of such changes, for in those days the only means of mass communication were the newspapers and these themselves were hampered by archaic customs and procedures with the result that they continued to portray life as largely uneventful and tranquil, or so it seems to us today. They reported few if any of the extraordinary changes that were imminent, often overlooking or ignoring the advances in politics and science that were finally to destroy this atmosphere of peace for ever.

Even a brief list of these changes must include the advent of cinema photography, the inauguration of the all-electric central London underground railway system with its fare of tuppence for any distance travelled, or the sudden popularity of the gramophone in 1900 – the same year in which Guglielmo Marconi was experimenting with wireless transmissions. The Royal Navy was to accept its first 'submersible torpedo-boat' in October 1901 and Elgar was about to commence work on the first of his 'Pomp and Circumstance' marches. In Britain, cars were to be properly licensed and numbered, while over the Channel Professor and Madame Curie were to introduce the world to radium in 1903, the year that the Wright brothers first flew, and Captain Scott was engaged on his first Antarctic expedition.

Still living too were such stalwarts of an earlier age as Florence Nightingale, heroine of England's Crimean War against Russia of 1854, and William Booth, founder in 1865 of the Salvation Army, an organisation which had developed into an immense power for compassion and good, while Robert Baden-Powell, a hero of the Boer War of the opening years of the century, was honing the organisation of his Boy Scout movement. The *Titanic*, doomed to pass into tragic history in 1912, was still under construction, while London was to see the abandonment of the last horse-drawn omnibus on Route 32, which ran from London Bridge to Moorgate. These were some of the events that shaped the world of the new twentieth century in which mankind was at last to conquer the skies.

Eugene B. Ely in a Curtiss biplane takes off from USS *Birmingham*, fitted with a special platform for the purpose on the advice of Glen Curtiss. This was the world's first take-off from a ship. The date was 14 November 1910. On 19 January 1911, Ely made the first landing on a vessel, USS *Pennsylvania*.

ONE

FAMILY

Father brought home a small toy, activated by a rubber spring that would lift itself up into the air. We built a number of copies of this toy which flew successfully.

Orville Wright, 1920

Milton and Susan Wright were married on 24 November 1861 and had five children (seven if one counts twins Ida, who died at birth on 7 March 1870, and Otis, who lived for only three days). The eldest child was Reuchlin (pronounced Rooshlin), who was born on 17 March 1861; he was followed by Lorin, born on 18 November 1862. These two were both of retiring temperament, in adulthood becoming successful farmers. Next came Wilbur on 6 April 1867 and Orville on 17 August 1871, a pair described at the time as 'absolutely inseparable'. Shortly before his early death, Wilbur described just how close the brothers were: 'From the time we were little children my brother Orville and myself lived together, played together, worked together and, in fact, thought together. We usually owned all our toys in common, talked over our thoughts and aspirations, so that nearly everything that was done in our lives has been the result of conversations, suggestions and discussions between us.' Neither was to marry, so that ninety years after the pair's historic achievement the only members of the family to remain were their nephew and niece, Horace and Ivonette, both resident in Dayton, Ohio, and Harold, Susan, Wilkinson and Marion Wright.

The only surviving daughter among Milton and Susan's children was Katherine, a girl of singular intelligence and ability. Born on 19 August 1874, she enjoyed an especially close relationship with Orville, who called her 'Swes' or 'Ster' ('*Schwesterchen*' meaning 'little sister'). Wilbur was frequently referred to as 'Ullam' (i.e. 'Jullam' – William) except by Orville who, unable to pronounce his brother's name properly as a small child, resorted to 'Bubbo' or 'Bubs' (meaning brother). The only member of the family to hold a college degree, Katherine married Henry J. Haskell in November 1926; sadly she died of pneumonia in 1929.

The four boys were all given uncommon Christian names, since their father thus hoped to distract attention from what he secretly thought was a somewhat commonplace surname. Katherine was named after the children's maternal grandmother, the child of Dutch-born Margaret Van Cleve, of seventeenth-century descent, married to innkeeper George Reeder. Milton in turn was the son of Catharine and her husband Dan Wright, and was born in an Indiana log cabin on 17 November 1828.

In this close and largely happy family there is little doubt that Susan, three years younger than her husband, was the parent with the greater influence, for although she was sickly, quiet and shy she was nevertheless determined and loyal, possessing a surprising mechanical turn of mind and even practical ability, rarely encouraged among women in that era. At the time of her marriage to Milton, he was a graduate of a theological college. Certificated to preach by the Church of the United Brethren, he was then teaching under the supervision of the Church, a fact that goes some way to explaining Wilbur's unsatisfied early ambition. Milton became a fully qualified schoolmaster, but two years after the birth of his third son he was appointed editor of the Brethren's weekly publication, the *Religious Telescope*, which required the family to move to Dayton. Here Milton purchased 7 Hawthorn Street while it was still under construction.

For the children this was the period when they received the grounding of what was to be a good education; in addition to basic subjects, they studied trigonometry, geometry and Greek, at which Wilbur excelled. At home too the books in Milton's collection were a source of fascination and the boys were able to indulge their growing natural talent for matters mechanical, inventing such diverse items as a paper folder (useful for the weekly church newspaper) and even a hay baler! They also helped remodel the rooms, constructing an enlarged front porch and building a new fireplace for the parlour. Music was enjoyed for relaxation. Orville, whose forte was for stringed instruments, played both the guitar and the mandolin. Both boys were members of a local choir and Wilbur is remembered as having 'a fine, bass voice'. He was also a gifted performer on the mouth organ, while Katherine excelled on the guitar.

But on 4 July 1889 tragedy struck the Wright family when Susan died. During her illness Wilbur kept a near-permanent vigil at his mother's bedside, although suffering himself from the lingering results of a nasty mishap while playing shinney (a rudimentary form of hockey on ice, usually known as shinty

right family home at 7 Hawthorn Street, Dayton. Orville was born here and Wilbur died at this address. The pair are believed to have been involved in the construction of the porch.
tesy of Special Collections and Archives, Wright State University, Ohio)

in Scotland and the north of England). An accidental blow from a bat had knocked out all his upper front teeth, which more than anything else led him to abandon his hopes of becoming a teacher. With Susan's death and the departure of Reuchlin and Lorin to set up their own married homes, the Wright household changed for ever.

Wilbur Wright who was the driving force, at least initially, in the brothers' search for man's flight at the close of the nineteenth century. *(Bruce Robertson Collection)*

It is always tempting to see historic personalities as little more than pasteboard figures, ignoring the fact that they were real flesh and blood individuals like ourselves. So what were they like, this pair who were foremost in changing the world? Wilbur, he of the slow, deliberate speech, was kindly, calm and thoughtful, with a habit of hesitating before speaking as if weighing up what he was about to say to make quite sure it was correct. He stood 5 feet 9¼ inches tall but his bony and angular build made him appear taller than he really was, and he weighed only some 120 lb. His hair was darker than that of his younger brother, and his strong features were dominated by a long nose and blue-grey eyes.

Orville, by contrast, was shorter than his elder brother, although only by an inch and a half, but he was much the heavier of the pair, turning the scales at

140 lb. He had reddish hair and a moustache over rather thin lips, and friends were initially struck by his unusually small hands. In temperament he was an optimist, an enthusiast who always looked on the bright side of life; and he was blessed with a swift, enquiring mind.

In a world where heavier-than-air flight was unknown, Wilbur and Orville would make the first such flight of some twelve seconds' duration in 1903, covering a distance of some 120 feet. Five years later they were able to make a flight of 80 miles, lasting three hours, as well as being able to execute banking turns and fly in controlled figure-of-eight patterns. Small wonder that one observer was moved to comment, 'Compared with Wright, we are as children', while another more far-sighted, remarked that here was 'a power which will control the fate of nations'.

But all this still lay in the future when Wilbur and Orville took their first steps in business with an attempt to create a printing enter-

Orville Wright who made a substantial contribution to the quest for heavier-than-air flight and survived into the twentieth century to see the results of his and his brother's work transform the world. *(Courtesy of Special Collections and Archives, Wright State University, Ohio)*

prise. The foundations for this interest had been laid long ago when the pair had experimented with childish printing sets. Later, when more realistic measures were attempted that called for genuine printing methods, a problem was encountered when their store of type proved insufficient for their requirements. Looking for ways to overcome their difficulty, Orville hit upon the idea of making an impression of each page in papier-mâché so that the type thus freed could be redistributed for further use. Over the next few years they would issue several publications, Wilbur settling into the role of writer and Orville that of printer. Their work proved popular in the small Dayton community where it was distributed, although the brothers made no profit, regarding themselves lucky if they managed so much as to break even.

This was the period when a new sport became all the rage. Cycling caught the public imagination as a result of the introduction of the safety bicycle in about 1880. This innovation replaced the earlier prototype's two wheels of different diameter with a pair of equal size, with the result that 'bicycling' developed into something of a craze in Europe and America. Perhaps that explains why so many pioneers of flight are recorded as being enthusiastic cyclists; it was the same youthful energy which translated itself into a burning desire for the novelty, freedom and movement of flight.

James Starley with nephew John and H.J. Lawson all founded a craze for 'safety bicycles' with two wheels of similar size to replace such types as the one seen here between 1874 and 1898. It attracted not only the Wrights, but also many other flying enthusiasts.
(Elmbridge Museum, Weybridge)

History does not record how the Wright brothers became acquainted with the new leisure machine after its introduction from Europe, but it certainly made a deep impression on Orville. Eager to own one, in 1882 he disposed of the old high-wheel cycle which had been his since he borrowed $3 from Wilbur to purchase it. In its place he bought a 'safety machine' which cost him $160, and he quickly became a cycle racing enthusiast. Six months later Wilbur joined him, using a second-hand machine procured at auction for half what his brother had paid. He soon became the leader, although he proved cautious, probably still troubled by his shinty accident.

That year the brothers decided that the new craze for cycling promised greater rewards than the meager income of their printing and publishing business and so the Wright Cycle Company was formed, its activities restricted initially to the sale of machines. At first trading in the new enterprise was slow, rent having to be paid for the premises they hired

One of several shops to sell cycles set up by the Wrights was this one at 1127 West Third Street, Dayton, which is the left of this pair. *(Courtesy of Special Collections and Archives, Wright State University, Ohio)*

from December at 1005 West Third Street. The printing enterprise was not totally abandoned, however, with Orville crossing the road to the earlier shop when trading permitted where his former business was now shared with Ed Sines, a friend of some years. The bicycle business proved eminently successful, so that repairing cycles was now added to their activities. The expansion of business called for a move to a new shop further along the street at No. 1034. Another change of address soon followed, this time to 22 South William Street in 1897, then to 1127 West Third Street where they traded from the left-hand of a pair of shops built into the front of a former house (the right-hand shop was the place of business of one of Dayton's undertakers). All these premises were near home.

The brothers' business now included the sale, repair and even design of their own brand of safety cycles. This last venture had blossomed almost by accident

The first camp set up by the Wrights for their flying experiments on the desolate Kill Devil Hills was a tented affair. Here Wilbur cleans a saucepan outside after a meal in 1900. *(Courtesy of Special Collections and Archives, Wright State University, Ohio)*

as a means of disposing of a pair of worthless high-wheel machines by constructing a tandem, the front and rear halves of which were joined with a hinge enabling its rider to sample the exciting and certainly dangerous sport of racing the contraption. They also invented a mechanical calculator and a new species of typewriter, and developed a type of front fork to accommodate pneumatic tyres for bicycles. In addition, they devised an economical system whereby a petrol motor could be harnessed to both lathe and drill in the engineering shop. Such work was usually done in the winter when business was slack, but it serves to illustrate the Wright brothers' burgeoning ingenuity.

The first of the Wright-designed bicycles, introduced when the pair were still trading from Williams Street, was named the Van Cleve after their Dutch ancestor; it was followed by the St Clair, which in turn was succeeded by the cheapest model of all, the $18 Wright Special. Assistance in the cycle workshop came from Charles Taylor whom the brothers had known from school days. They took him into their employment in 1901 and it is from him that it is possible to gain some insight into Wilbur and Orville's reasons for never marrying. He believed that Wilbur's frequent explanation – that he had no time for a wife – was probably true. However, it was clear that the ever-courteous Wilbur was abnormally shy of marriageable young women, and some writers have even been tempted to speculate whether he had a foreboding that his life would suddenly be cut short. Certainly, he had received a warning of mortality in November 1892 when he suffered an attack of appendicitis. At the time it was a serious condition, anaesthetics being primitive and the operation dangerous, so that the doctor could do little more than advise a bland diet as well as keeping warm. Luckily, Wilbur recovered.

Like Wilbur, Orville too never married, probably because he also was excessively shy, a state of affairs no doubt exacerbated by the fact that good and in many ways enlightened as Milton was, people outside their immediate circle were regarded by the family with caution if not suspicion. Even so, a tradition existed that Orville had proposed to one of Katherine's friends – and been rejected, perhaps on religious grounds.

Meanwhile, after the initial boom, by 1894 the bicycle business was being described as only 'fair'. However, in view of the fact that three other cycle shops existed in the township, trading was by no means unhealthy.

In 1902, the brothers enjoyed the luxury of a wood-framed building to augment the tent, the former seen here under construction beside the tent which was the brothers' original accommodation. This view emphasises the desolation of the spot. *(Courtesy of Special Collections and Archives, Wright State University, Ohio)*

Nevertheless, the Wright brothers decided that turnover could be improved, regarding conditions as 'a little slack' and so devoted more attention to the still-functioning printing concern. But the enormous effort both put into the twin enterprises took up a great deal of time and demanded much energy, leaving them physically drained a year later, with little to show for it.

However, as is often the way of business, progress is seldom marked by a single, dramatic leap forward and it was 1898 before they considered themselves established; they were 'very busy' selling, repairing and manufacturing cycles. Their success contained an element of luck, probably due to their location. Dayton was busy but by no means a centre of commerce; elsewhere the bicycle boom had already peaked, the market was saturated, and it was clear that the best years had passed.

The comparative downturn fed Wilbur's sense of being trapped. He felt himself unqualified for business, commenting, 'The boys of the Wright family are all lacking in determination and push.' Indeed, although these thoughts

The Wrights' first glider, built in 1900, seen here while being flown as a kite. Lost in mid-October, it was wrecked by the wind, being flung some 20 feet and damaged beyond repair. *(Courtesy of Special Collections and Archives, Wright State University, Ohio)*

were addressed to another member of the family, and probably intended to include all the male Wrights, it seems that the old sense of urgency was again coming to the surface since, as a modern biographer points out, the years between 1885 and 1899 had marked a period when Wilbur had allowed life to pass him by, taking the easy path. Yet there were times when he still believed that the best was yet to come. Clearly, the profession of teacher still beckoned.

The reason for this period of self-analysis is not difficult to discover. The Wright household was quieter than brothers Wilbur and Orville had ever known it. Their father Milton, now elevated to the dignity of a bishop of the Church of the United Brethren, was away from home for lengthy periods as his calling demanded much visiting of outlying churches. Then something happened. Katherine, who was now teaching, was about to leave home at the end of the vacation when Orville was suddenly taken ill. He quickly fell into a delirium, his temperature exceeding 105° C. He was diagnosed with typhus, an emergency sufficient for Milton to return home and assist his daughter and son in nursing Orville. Gradually the fever broke, although the accompanying hallucinations did not cease for considerably longer. Orville missed the local civic celebrations to which he had been looking forward; for six weeks he was too weak to rise from his bed. When he finally did so, it was in a home of which he and Wilbur would soon be the only occupants, Katherine returned to her work late and Milton resumed his travels, his mind at ease now that the crisis had passed for his son.

This incident left a lasting impression on Wilbur's troubled mind and contributed in no small way to his own disquiet. Reminded again of mortality, Orville's experience had a subtle effect on his own thinking, doubtless reinforced by the discovery, during bedside readings to his stricken brother, that the German experimenter Lilienthal had died. He was killed during one of his glider trials, news that in turn rekindled Wilbur's own interest in mankind's search for a means of mechanical flight, an interest that had remained dormant since the childhood gift of the toy helicopter the pair had received from their father.

In part, Orville's recovery – literally from the jaws of death – meant a return to the happy atmosphere the brothers had enjoyed when they had been the only occupants of their home. That was the time when the brothers had displayed an interest and skill in cooking, an art in which Wilbur was the more adventurous, striving to provide a varied diet, the two taking turns in alternate weeks to prepare the three meals a day. Mealtimes would have provided ample opportunity for the young men, now in their mid-to-late twenties, to discover

Kill Devil Hills, 1902. This view shows the 100-foot Big Hill with West Hill, 40 feet lower, in the foreground. *(Courtesy of Special Collections and Archives, Wright State University, Ohio)*

The Wrights' 1901 glider, a bold tailless design that in some ways anticipated the much later canard principles. Capable of very slow speed using rising air currents, it was believed to be able to remain airborne for hours in the right air currents. *(Courtesy of Special Collections and Archives, Wright State University, Ohio)*

rs Dan Tate and E.C. Huffaker prepare to launch the 1901 glider into a stiff headwind. This was the usual method of becoming airborne during this period. *(Courtesy of Special* *·tions and Archives, Wright State University, Ohio)*

that they shared a certain nagging lack of fulfilment. Wilbur felt that life was passing him by with little to show for it; Orville suffered from a similar sense of frustration. Having played an active part in establishing their printing business, he now found no job satisfaction in his duties there; the manager, Ed Sines, was proving entirely competent. Yet the old yearnings were as strong as ever; what new fields were jointly open to the two?

Fred Kelly, the semi-official biographer of the Wrights who wrote and researched with the permission of Orville, tells how the answer was to come quite unexpectedly one day in the summer of 1896. The pair were engaged in casual conversation with Cordy Ruse, a friend who had been employed part time in the bicycle shop. The subject of their discussion was one which fascinated the folk of Dayton, the 'horseless carriage' which Ruse had constructed and in which he could frequently be seen on the town's streets, his contraption emitting strange mechanical noises, throwing out clouds of odorous fumes and probably frightening the horses. Orville in particular was fascinated by the machine while Wilbur clearly regarded automobiles as little more than a subject for jest.

'I've just thought of a wonderful invention!' he cried, slapping his thigh and startling the group of young men. 'All there is to it is a bed sheet to be fastened

Under a lowering sky, the 1902 glider with twin rudders is flown off the slope of Big Kill Devil Hill by Wilbur on 2 October. *(Courtesy of Special Collections and Archives, Wright State University, Ohio)*

1902 glider in single-rudder configuration photographed by Lorin Wright on a visit to the camp site on 10 October with (left to right): Octave Chanute, Orville and Wilbur Wright, Herring, George A. Spratt and Dan Tate. At the end of the season about 250 glides were made in two days with this machine, although the best time in the air was only about seconds covering some 622 feet. *(Courtesy of Special Collections and Archives, Wright State University, Ohio)*

beneath the automobile to catch all the bolts, nuts and other parts that'll keep falling off!' – a joke that sounds very like an English one about the firm that supplied a free squirrel with each of its cars to follow behind and pick up all the dropped nuts. But the possibility of breaking into the new trade which he saw must replace the bicycle craze took root in Orville's mind so that in 1897 he suggested to Wilbur that they enter the motorcar production business. But his brother rejected the idea, allegedly with the words: 'Why, it would be easier to build a flying machine!'

The Wright brothers had just taken the first small step on the road that would make them foremost among the men who changed the world.

TWO

ADVANCES

*I am certain I can reach a point much in advance of any previous
workers in this field even if success is not attained just at the moment.*
Wilbur Wright, 1900

The years between 1896 and 1899 were quiet ones for the Wright
brothers. Their bicycle business had settled down from its initial frenzy
and still provided them with an acceptable income. Their interest in
aviation had been relegated to the back of their minds, where it remained
dormant until it was suddenly reawakened in the early spring of the final year
of the nineteenth century, when the pair chanced to browse through a book on
ornithology. His enthusiasm renewed, the now 33-year-old Wilbur, ever keen to
obtain his information from the best sources, wrote what was to prove a
momentous letter to the Smithsonian Institution; in it he requested that they
suggest books suitable for extending the pair's knowledge of flight.

Dated 30 May 1899, the letter outlined their boyhood experiments and
continued, '. . . my observations have since convinced me that human flight is
possible and practicable,' and expressed a wish 'if possible to add my mite to
help on the future worker who will attain final success'. He concluded: 'I am an
enthusiast, but not a crank in the sense that I have some pet theories as to the
proper construction of a flying machine.' The reply listed five relevant article
titles and suggested another three names for further reading. Of these, the
brothers would have been particularly attracted by the work of the late and still
much admired Otto Lilienthal; another was by Octave Chanute, to whom
Wilbur would write almost a year later.

The Wrights were now confident that their bicycle business could finance
their own aviation tests. Anxious to approach their new endeavour
methodically, the two decided first to augment their entirely theoretical
knowledge with some practical experiments. They felt that the best way of
gaining this experience was by the construction of a kite. Completed in August

The spot chosen by the Wrights for their flying experiments since it offered space and a reliable prevailing wind. Wilbur reached Kitty Hawk on 13 September 1900, commenting 'We came down here for wind and sand, and we have got them!' (*Author*)

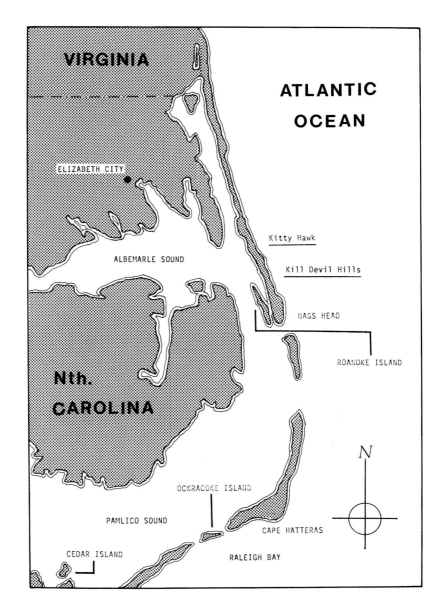

1899, it was relatively small with a wingspan of only 5 feet. The brothers proposed to control it from the ground using the wing-warping system, a method of 'warping' or twisting the extremities of the wings to perform the work later done by ailerons which were not in vogue at the time. The combined wing cells were capable of moving fore and aft, their connection to an elevator (then confusingly termed a 'horizontal rudder') at the same time altering its angle, being automatic as a result.

It may well have been their adoption of wing-warping that gave rise to the belief that much of the Wrights' understanding of aerodynamics was gained from the study of bird flight. Years later this was refuted by Orville: 'Learning the secret of flight from a bird was a good deal like learning the secret of magic from a magician. After you know the trick and what to look for, you can see the thing you didn't notice when you did not know exactly what to look for.' Even so, it is a fact that their adoption of wing-warping owed something to a memory of the landing behaviour of buzzards.

To control their first flying craft which had wings of only 15 inches chord the pair worked out a system using a series of cords. Two were attached to the tips at the leading edge of the wings on one side, the others similarly attached on that opposite. One pair of cords from each side was fastened to opposite ends of a stick held in the operator's hands, so that he could incline or 'warp' the angles of the leading edges of the wing-tips, thus changing the lift and causing the tips to rise or drop. The spectacle of Wilbur trying to control his airborne kite from the ground never ceased to attract the attention of Dayton's citizens and, accompanied by a throng of local boys, he would test fly the kite from a common on the outskirts of town. Soon, successful flights with this kite prompted the Wrights to contemplate something rather more ambitious – eventually a prototype capable of carrying the weight of a man. When the day-to-day demands of the bicycle business permitted, their decision to make such an attempt was communicated to no less a personage than Octave Chanute, in a letter from Wilbur dated 13 May 1900.

Chanute, then aged sixty-eight, was a prosperous, witty, French-speaking American. Until recently he had specialised in railway development, as his earlier writings confirmed, but he had also interested himself in the problems of flight. To this end he had constructed several gliders that had been tested on the shores of Lake Michigan. Drawn together by their shared enthusiasm, it did not take long for their correspondence to develop into personal visits which in turn produced a firm friendship between the three.

Drawing on the experience of his own experiments, Chanute now advised that the new glider which they proposed to construct – the brothers' first foray into practical aerodynamics – should retain the earlier biplane form and employ the Pratt wing truss form rather than that of the bird-like planform monoplanes such as had been favoured by Lilienthal, among others. But this was the only piece of technical advice for which the brothers were beholden to Chanute. Their immediate concern was to discover a suitable spot from which trial flights of their planned man-lifting kite could be carried out, free from the

...te continually refined his ideas for gliders and produced this version in 1900. The span was about 22 feet but the idea persisted of the operator hanging through the lower centre-section ...eing kept in place by padded arm supports. *(Bruce Robertson Collection)*

attentions of onlookers and with sufficient space. Reliable winds were also an important prerequisite.

Once more, it was Wilbur who, seeking the best reference sources for his information, made the necessary enquiries, this time to the US Weather Bureau in Washington. The reply he received proved unexpectedly valuable, containing as it did detailed lists for the months of September and October which were especially interesting. Chicago seemed to be the windiest city with speeds averaging only a little under 17 miles per hour. Attractive as this seemed, Wilbur immediately rejected it – he had no wish for their flying investigations to become a subject of entertainment for a major centre of population. An alternative had to be found.

Kitty Hawk, North Carolina, a place of which he had never heard, sounded a more likely spot. Here, wind speeds averaged in excess of 13 miles per hour with even higher speeds occasionally being registered. So in early August 1900, a letter sent directly to the weather station there brought a most promising reply – the proposed location had a stretch of sand about 1 mile deep and 5 miles wide, clear of all obstructions. In the centre lay a hill 80 feet or more high which, like the area as a whole, was bare of trees. Clearly this was the spot. Bleak it certainly was, but there was a Life Saving (lifeboat) Station about a mile distant and the brothers could be accommodated in tents until something more substantial was constructed. In the meantime, their most pressing responsibility was to organise the running of the bicycle shop in their absence.

When their business arrangements had been completed, they turned their attention to acquiring the necessary materials for the construction of the man-

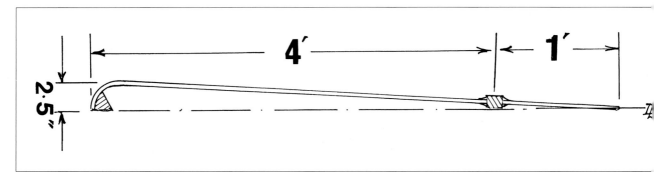

A representative example of a unique type of wing section, the culmination of the Wrights' refinement for a glider design. Their originality of approach was thus evident even in the days their earliest experiments once a promising airframe concept had been evolved. Wing ribs were of ash, bent to form a type of curved leading edge which was strengthened with a length roughly triangular-section white pine, the same being used for a 'rear spar', but of rectangular section. The whole was then covered with sateen and, as Wilbur was to explain, 'an extra of cloth ran up and over it [the rear spar] to lessen resistance'. (*Author*)

carrying glider. It was decided that some of the preliminary work would be carried out at home in Dayton, the remainder at Kitty Hawk.

It was the evening of 6 September when Wilbur boarded the train from Union Station. Breaks in the journey in attempts to purchase the larger items from which to construct the glider and the fact that even when he was only a short distance from Kitty Hawk, no one seemed to know how to get there, plus the ensuing delay in finding a boatman, meant it was 13 September before he finally arrived and found lodgings. Ten days later he was able to report to his father that the glider was 'nearly finished'. The machine had a span of 17 feet and a wing area of 165 square feet; it made its first flight as an unmanned kite soon after the brothers (Orville had now joined Wilbur) had set up camp on the edge of the desolate dunes.

Wright gliders, after the brothers' success in evolving a powered machine, were produced in a number of modified forms in many countries, the Clarke-Wright type, advertised here, being available in England. These were usually sold as initial trainers. The prices and the continued mention of a 'Chanute Type, body control' are of interest. (*Author's collection*)

The idea of the moving wing cell had now been abandoned and the horizontal surface which had previously acted as a tail was moved to the front in the belief that it would now provide better pitch control. Although the former system of wing-warping was retained, it soon became clear that the pronounced dihedral which it was hoped would ensure lateral stability would have to be reduced and the structure rerigged. Unfortunately, No. 1 glider crashed on 10 October sustaining damage that took three days to repair. Nevertheless Wilbur had managed to fly it once, an experience that confirmed his feelings that an unmanned series was still necessary.

However, winter was approaching and survival now became their priority, for their location was exposed to winds from the north-east blowing at around 45 miles per hour, shifting the sand in such quantities that visibility was no better than in a dense fog. Yet the brothers' fascination for exploring the mysteries of flight proved so compelling that it was only after the pressing appeals of the locals, anxious for their safety, that they agreed to move. They drew some comfort from the fact that they had achieved unmanned but controlled flights of appreciable length.

Encouraged by their success, it is small wonder that having devoted the spring and summer of 1901 to their bicycle business, the Wrights planned to spend longer in North Carolina. September and October saw tests with a more ambitious glider and the setting up of a permanent camp at Kill Devil Hills. They built a shed to house the machine whose design had been completed by mid-May.

The span of this glider was to measure 22 feet with a chord of 7 feet and an area of 290 square feet. They intended the pilot to remain prone throughout, a difference from the planned procedure for the pilot of No. 2 glider who was supposed to sit up for a landing. The wing camber was now 1:12 with an anhedral of 4 inches at the tips. Cables attached to a pivoted T-bar allowed the pilot to operate the wing-warping with his feet.

The fact that the brothers appear to have given this No. 2 glider its first outing in July indicates not only their awareness of the significance of their experiments but also their confidence in the arrangements for the all-important bicycle business which was being supervised by their old friend Charles Taylor.

The Kill Devil Hills, lying about 4 miles south of Kitty Hawk where the first tests had taken place, were chosen for the trials with the 1901 glider. Straight away the glider was tested with a pilot. They were severely disappointed when the pronounced camber of the wings resulted in excessive travel of the centre of pressure (i.e. the point of intersection of the aerodynamic force of an aerofoil and its chord); only when the angle of incidence was changed (that between the chord line of an aerofoil and the direction of the airflow) was a satisfactory performance achieved. In a wind blowing at some 27 miles per hour glides of up to 389 feet were obtained by what was the brothers' largest flying machine to date. All the flying on this glider was carried out by Wilbur.

The brothers had left for Kitty Hawk on Sunday 7 July 1901, only arriving on the evening of the following Thursday. They were held up by one of the most severe storms ever recorded for the area, weather which still made work outside inadvisable though their only shelter was a tent. Describing the reason for their delay, Wilbur noted cryptically that the 'Anemometer cups gave way at 93 miles per hour' and 'after a dry spell of seven weeks the storm was followed by rains for a full week'. Worse was to come; when their assistant Edward Huffaker arrived the following Thursday afternoon he brought with him 'a swarm of mosquitoes which came in a mighty cloud, almost darkening the sun'.

The first of a programme of seventeen flights with the 1901 glider was made on Saturday 27 July from the Big Hill. Initially the machine refused to act like that of the previous year, although on one occasion it climbed 'higher and higher until it finally came to a stop at a height variously estimated as . . . between 18 and 40 feet'. Orville subsequently commented, 'This is the very fix Lilienthal got into when he was killed.' Later the machine pancaked from a height of 20 feet without injury to Wilbur or damage to itself; the elevator in front prevented it nosing over or falling on to one wing.

The brothers struck camp on 28 August, earlier than they had intended. The weather was rapidly deteriorating and the locals assured them that there was no chance of better conditions until the following year. Resigned, the pair packed up, their feelings mixed on the progress they had made. Temporarily disheartened, Wilbur confided to Orville during the train journey that he thought it would be a thousand years before mankind flew. But once back in the familiar surroundings of home they could take a more balanced view of the summer's work, agreeing that there was now good reason to distrust the calculations of earlier experimenters which they had previously accepted without question; Lilienthal's air pressure tables were particularly in doubt. There could be other explanations, perhaps including miscalculations, for the alarming tendency No. 2 glider had shown for its positively warped wing to swing back, flinging the entire aircraft round so that it side-slipped and crashed, but, Wilbur concluded, 'having set out with absolute faith in our existing scientific data, we were driven to doubt one thing or another, till finally, after two years of experiment, we cast all aside, and decided to rely entirely on our own investigations'. At first they attempted to do this with the aid of specimen aerofoils fastened to the front of cycles pedalled furiously along the local streets, later resorting to tests in a simple wind tunnel (which they constructed from a discarded starch box), the readings confirming their suspicions. Moreover, they made a meticulous record of their work, unfailingly photographing all their trials with the simple cameras of the period and later developing and printing each set of exposures.

Despite their disappointment with the results obtained from flying No. 2 glider, the period between September 1901 and August 1902 – one of the longest unbroken periods of tests they had been able to carry out to date – was also to be one of their most intensive. Armed as they now were with figures determined with the aid of their new wind tunnel, these not so much disproving the figures on which they had depended which came from Lilienthal's trials, but rather supporting their own results from observing the behaviour of a flat plate. Once the Wrights had satisfied themselves on this point, it was only a short step to realising that if allowance was made for the fact that these tables could be taken as about 60 per cent accurate for an aerofoil surface, it was possible to forecast the likely behaviour of one such and design it to function for a specific purpose.

The new glider introduced in 1902 was therefore the first equipped with the scientific features Wilbur and Orville had long sought to incorporate, the machine notching up almost one thousand test flights from the Kill Devil Hills in the fall of 1902. Now a new confidence was reflected in the design. Although almost exactly following the original pattern, with the foreplane and tail unit still set uncomfortably close to the wing cell, and although the span was comparatively large at 32 feet 1 inch with a chord of 5 feet and a camber of 1:25, while the machine was still being built Wilbur noted with enthusiasm that 'The indications are that it will glide on an angle of about 7° to 8° instead of 9° to 10° as last year'.

Control was still by means of wing-warping, operated by the pilot's movements as he lay prone across a cradle from which wires operated the rear tips of the main flying surfaces; these surfaces had an anhedral as on the earlier gliders and a similar forward elevator. The large pair of rectangular fins at the rear were an innovation, however. The brothers believed that these surfaces would function as a form of weather-vane, counteracting the tendency of a wing to swing back under the effect of a tip warped upwards, retain lateral balance and prevent the glider side-slipping and crashing if control was lost. It was clear, therefore, that the doubling of the vertical surfaces had only

The twin controls of an early biplane are seen here demonstrated by much-loved actress, singer and flying enthusiast Pauline Chase. On 13 February 1911 she made a significant flight over Southport with pioneer flyer Grahame White, although her very first flight appears to have been in the early spring of 1910. *(Author's collection)*

An early Maurice Farman being flown by Legagneux in 1910. Like the Wrights, Henry Farman, Englishman living in France, had been caught up in the world's cycling craze of the 1890s. He became France's leading aviator in January 1908 making Europe's first circular flight at Issy, although the zenith of the Farman brothers' flying achievement would come a few years (Bruce Robertson Collection)

increased their problems, rather than the other way round. In an effort to remedy matters, a single surface was introduced to replace the trouble-inducing pair, the control cables of the new single surface also running to the pilot's cradle and enabling No. 3 glider to be smoothly banked in its modified form. Their initial reaction had been to increase the angle of the dihedral, dropping the wing-tips to as much as 5 inches below the horizontal. But it was Orville's work on the tail which finally improved matters; the idea occurred to him 'while lying awake . . . [when he] studied out a new vertical rudder, the new single component having a surface area of 6 square feet'.

Pleased as the brothers were with this fresh run of success, it was clear even by the third week in August that the demands they were making on themselves were at a heavy cost; Katherine commented, 'Will is thin . . . and nervous and so is Orv . . . [yet] they think Kitty Hawk cures all ills.'

It is little wonder that their health was suffering. In addition to the strains of flying a glider whose reactions they only half understood, they were taking upon themselves not only the repair of their storm-damaged camp, but were extending it, as well as erecting a larger shed to protect the new machine. They were now able to predict the glider's performance with the aid of the wind tunnel, one of the best glides being for a distance of 622 feet 6 inches with a duration of 26 seconds. This was the brothers' best and, for the present, final glider design. The machine is believed to have clocked up a total of between 700 and 1,000 flights in a period of six weeks, with many days lost due to rain. Although not all flights were recorded, the brothers' modesty and careful scientific methods are reflected in the cautious statement, 'A thousand glides is equivalent to about four hours of steady practice – far too little to give anyone a complete mastery of the art of flying.' Nevertheless, the intensity of the pair's test programme is reflected in the fact that of the total, 375 glides were made in the last six days of the trials.

Their attitude to their self-imposed task was set out by Wilbur a month after the programme's close: 'The prime object of these experiments was to obtain practice in the management of a man-carrying machine, but an object of scarcely less importance was to obtain data for the study of the scientific problems involved in flight.' It was as well that this gruelling series of tests had been undertaken while they were based in a camp that was almost 'luxurious' by comparison with the primitive horrors of their earlier accommodation. Now they had a two-storey shack with their sleeping quarters upstairs and room for

arman type Circuit aeroplane that appeared during 1911. *(Bruce Robertson Collection)*

Wilbur, seen here in the gloom of one of the two sheds that now dominated their site at Kitty Hawk, working on the 'Flyer' which still had to be assembled. As 1903 began its final quarter, the world at large, and indeed even the Wrights, was unaware that it was to be changed for ever, materially, by the efforts of just two men. *(Courtesy of Special Collections and Archives, Wright State University, Ohio)*

visitors below, a meticulously laid out kitchen with canned foods arranged neatly on shelves along the top of one wall, each container with its label facing outwards; no matter that part of the floor space had to be shared with the partially dismantled 1901 glider. And there was a reliable source of fresh water to hand from a well, 16 feet deep, which the brothers had dug.

With the passage of time, Wilbur and Orville, assisted by, among others, Dan Tate, Augustus M. Herring, George A. Spratt and Ed Huffaker, made themselves comfortable against the punishing and almost unceasing winds which they had so assiduously sought. With a stove made from an old carbide can in the 'living room' and despite the fact that it was necessary to sit huddled on the floor to relish its heat while avoiding the smoke it gave off, they would read and discuss the latest issue of *Scientific American* to reach them.

The practice ground where the tests were conducted was nothing more than a level of bare sand with a number of hills that had been created by the unceasing wind that constantly re-formed their shape. These were known as 'Big Hill', which rose to about 100 feet, 'West Hill' with a height of 60 feet and the steep 'Little Hill', about half the height of the latter.

Since launching the gliders still relied entirely on manpower, the hills proved of great assistance in getting the gliders off and lifted by the wind. Orville described one such launch in his diary:

The early part of the glides were really soaring [gliding with the assistance of wind], our speed over the ground being from one to two feet per second, often for distances of 25 to 75 feet. We took a number of measurements of the relative wind by running along beside the machine with an anemometer. . . . Many of these flights were at heights from 40 to 60 feet, by far the highest gliding we had ever done.

Here a Henry Farman Type III makes a dramatic picture taking off, probably at Rheims. The alignment of the undercarriage possibly points to a semi-castoring undercarriage, popular at the time. (Author's collection)

Desolate as the camp was, friends and family would make the effort to visit the two men from time to time. Although it is possible to overstate the magnitude of the journeys, Americans are more ready to travel distances which seem prodigious by European standards. But the spirit of the early settlers was still active in the American character at the beginning of the twentieth century; Wilbur and Orville's brother Lorin was among those who made the journey to the bleak spot on the Atlantic coast, a spot familiar four hundred years earlier to Elizabethan explorers from England. Octave Chanute too was in the habit of joining the younger men at Kitty Hawk, apparently lending them the multi-wing glider he had used for his trials at the end of the nineteenth century.

When Wilbur and Orville finally left their testing ground at Kill Devil Hills in 1902 and returned to Dayton, it was with a sense of hopeful anticipation. What would the next year hold? Although it would see their bold and momentous step into the realms of powered flight, in 1911 Orville would return once more to make gliding trials at the old location.

Their departure was eventually to result in the formation of the Wright Company. With Wilbur as its president, and having first purchased Wright patents, this had been incorporated in November 1909 to build Wright aeroplanes in the USA. Indeed, the previous eleven months had seen the Wrights' company become the largest builder of flying machines in the world, capable of producing four machines a month. It boasted a display team which Orville went to Montgomery, Alabama in March to train, including among its pilots Frank Coffyn, a son of the Wrights' banker. Five years later, the Wright Company would be absorbed in the Wright–Martin merger; now, the aim of the early autumn move back to Kill Devil Hills was to test a new glider in October.

The glider to be tested was of an entirely new design with a span of 32 feet and an area of 300 square feet, and it is chiefly remembered because it was used to set up a world record on 24 October when it flew for 9 minutes and 45 seconds – an achievement that was not to be bettered for some ten years.

On its first appearance the glider presented with a fixed vertical fin in front of the wing leading edges at the mid-point of the aircraft and secured to the main spars. Later this was moved forward to the frontal point of a boom extending from the main spar of the lower wing to give the 1902 glider a truly singular appearance. In addition, it differed in having very shallow landing skids, a tall, rectangular rudder rigged within the apex of the end of the open girder construction, while a tailplane extended beyond it.

Accompanying Wilbur on this visit to the Kill Devil Hills was Alec Ogilvie, an Englishman who had already test-flown one of the first Short-built Wright

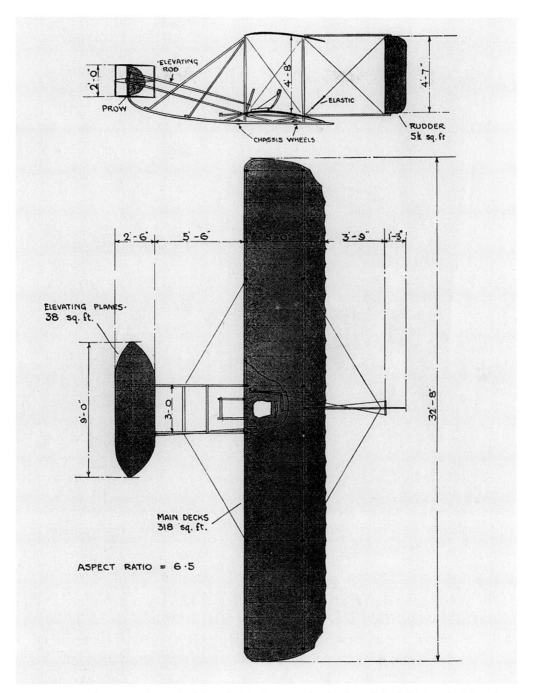

A contemporary general arrangement drawing of a Clarke-Wright glider. This type was based on the Wright No. 3 glider but with a biplane elevator and seat. A Clarke-Wright glider had been ordered by Alec Ogilvie (later closely associated with the Wrights) for him to learn to fly, and this was dispatched to Eastbourne at 1.15 p.m. on 28 July towed by a pair of motor cars, and arriving at 6.30 p.m., Ogilvie later recording, 'Next morning kit was put together and the same day several fine glides were made, some of them 12 feet above the ground', later adding, 'Soaring flights up to 343 yards were carried out last Sunday.' *Flight* reported: 'Mr Ogilvie is at present practising with his glider until such time as he obtains delivery of his full-sized Wright flyer.' *(The Flight Collection)*

The Wright biplane on which Alec Ogilvie qualified. He was eventually to obtain RAeC pilot's certificate No. 7 on 24 May 1910 at Camber Sands, Sussex, where this photograph was tak⬛

(Author's collection)

gliders in 1908, the same year in which he designed and built the Ogilvie Quadruplane Glider. This was fitted with a four-wheel undercarriage and was launched by being towed behind a car. Unfortunately, on one occasion the rope broke when the glider was at a height of about 30 feet and Alec's brother, who was acting as pilot, fell through the frail wings. Ogilvie also flew one of the first batch of Short-built Wright biplanes in Britain having become a self-taught pilot on 24 May 1910; he now used a Short-constructed Wright biplane powered by a 40-hp N.E.C. engine (the intended Wright-designed 30-hp Léon Bollée not being available when the machine was flown from Camber Sands, near Rye in Sussex); the biplane achieved the record-breaking flight of 139¾ miles in a time of 3 hours 55 minutes. This machine was moved to and from its hangar with the aid of a wheeled trolley and windlass. It was also here that Ogilvie founded a small flying school in 1912 with himself as the only instructor. Alas, history also records only one certificated pupil.

To gain experience of the Short-Wright before taking delivery, Ogilvie and T.P. Searight had ordered a Wright-type glider, known as the Clarke-Wright from T.W.K. Clarke & Company of 14 Union Street, Kingston-on-Thames, Surrey. This machine was based on the Wright No. 3 Type but with a biplane elevator in front and provision for the pilot to sit upright rather than lie prone. Its span was 32 feet 8 inches with a length of 18 feet; a fixed fin was fitted between the elevator surfaces, while the two-bay, warping wings were double-surfaced. Specially constructed in four weeks, this glider was delivered in August 1908 and launched from the beach at Eastbourne, Sussex, where its longest distance flown was 343 yards.

Like so many others of his generation, Alec Ogilvie was shortly to see service in the First World War, then only three years away. He was commissioned into the Royal Naval Air Service, joining the Admiralty Air Department's technical Section T.6 by 1916. A short time before, he had encouraged Richard Fairey to form his own aircraft manufacturing company.

But all these events lay in the future. Elated by the success of glider No. 3, the Wrights were scheduling the next series of experiments for 1903 and in March of the new year they applied for patent status to safeguard their discoveries – a patent that was not finally granted until 1906. Nevertheless, they now regarded themselves as sufficiently experienced and knowledgeable to face their greatest challenge – to build a powered flying machine. Not until June 1903 was the bold step taken to commence the construction of such a machine. From its appearance, future chroniclers would assume that it was nothing more than the glider of the previous year, fitted with a motor. There was certainly a resemblance between the two, but the historic aeroplane was of an entirely new design. Much hard work was called for in the coming months.

THREE

SUCCESS

When Orville and I began, we had no idea at all whether flying was going to be possible or not. But what we had made our minds up to do was to find out.

Wilbur Wright, 1908

The Wright brothers probably approached 1903 with mixed emotions; they believed that their success with the previous year's glider heralded the culmination or failure of their experiments. But if they felt excitement, they were nevertheless careful to maintain the steady, scientific methods that had served them so well, an approach that showed itself in their insistence on continued trials to find a reliable, lightweight engine.

Having decided that this must be a petrol motor – sometimes known as a 'light oil engine' at the time – they rejected the steam motors favoured by many of their contemporaries. Ten manufacturers were approached, the required motor being described as having to supply 8 to 9 hp and weigh no more than 180 lb. However, with the exception of one French company that offered a motor of the required horsepower and weighing only 135 lb, the manufacturers'

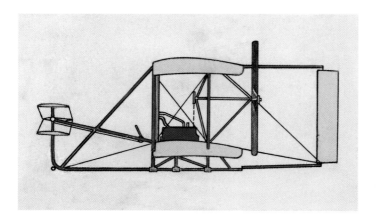

Resembling the gliders that had preceded it, the Wright 'Flyer' turned out to be a beautifully simple design compared with the complex products of some experimenters. Orville had made similar model gliders as a schoolboy and sold them to his friends. (*Author*)

attitude was less than enthusiastic, perhaps due to a wariness of getting involved with what was then still considered the foolish myth of mechanical flight. Unfortunately, even the French motor failed to meet their requirements since it had only a single cylinder with a 4-inch bore and a 5-inch stroke, and so the brothers resolved to design their own motor.

In this they were certainly helped and supported by Charles Taylor who had first joined the pair in their Dayton bicycle business. A first-class engineer, like his employers he was nevertheless totally inexperienced at building an engine, although they had all been responsible for the motor that drove the machine tools in the workshop of the bicycle business. The result of their endeavours was an aero-motor with four cylinders running in an aluminium crankcase, gravity fed and water-cooled. There was no carburettor, air passing instead through vapourised petrol to form a mixture that was detonated in the hot crankcase and fed directly to the inlet valves. The resultant motor, on which Orville and Charles began work in December 1902, ran particularly quietly for its type.

Lower on the Wrights' list of priorities was the question of propeller design. They had decided that a pair driven via sprocket chains in the manner of bicycle pedals was preferable to direct drive, since such a solution would permit a comparatively slow rate of rotation, although this in turn demanded a motor that ran without vibration otherwise the chains would have broken. After six weeks' work this little 12-hp motor first ran on 12 February 1903, although only the next day the crankcase shattered and a new one was needed. It was May before the motor could be assembled and run once more, and even then it still required a great deal of adjustment.

However, the design of propellers was a problem not previously encountered. The practice of other experimenters

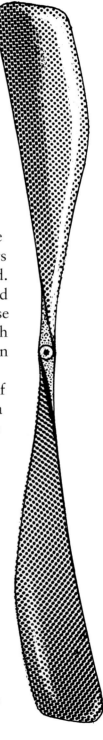

An example of a Wright propeller. These achieved something like 66 per cent efficiency since they were designed on the principle of a rotating aerofoil. Previously the best performance had been those of Langley and Maxim which had an efficiency of about 50 per cent, but these were fanbladed, similar to marine propellers, themselves only introduced in 1843. (*Author*)

whereby they emulated ships' screws proved useless since these literally 'screwed' themselves through the water; the propellers of a flying machine needed to emulate rotating wings, their thrust depending on the angle of a blade which in turn was dependent on the speed of rotation. Armed with this knowledge, the brothers commenced the design of their propellers to a new formula, quite different from that governing maritime screws. The results were a pair of pusher propellers for their machine that revolved in different directions by means of the twisting of one driving chain so avoiding the anticipated problem of torque (the forces operating on an airscrew blade in the opposite direction to that in which it rotates).

While this intensive work was in progress, time had to be found to devise a suitable aircaft and here the earlier glider trials were to prove invaluable. Although none of these machines was of any use if merely fitted with an engine, No. 3 glider provided a strong pointer to the direction they should take. The powered 'Flyer' (the brothers knew it as 'the whopper flying machine') differed

The historic take-off during the late morning of 17 December 1903. It covered 852 feet and lasted for 59 seconds with Orville at the controls and Wilbur alongside to steady the first stages of its rise from the launching rail. The trestle in the foreground is one of a pair used as supports of the machine at rest. *(Courtesy of Special Collections and Archives, Wright State University, Ohio)* from the most successful of the gliders in a number of fundamentals: it had double fabric surfaces to the wings which were covered in 'Pride of the West' muslin, a brand of cloth so tightly woven that it was felt it could be safely used without doping to fill the interstices; while the ribs were each made from two lengths of timber bent over a series of wooden blocks that acted as a jig, and then tacked and glued into shape; and the front and rear booms placed the fore and aft surfaces at distances from the wings which were to be increased in subsequent variants. The end bows of these, which needed to be bent upwards during manufacture, were made by a local Dayton firm whose usual expertise lay in the

The original 'Flyer' mounted on its launching rail, its rear towards the camera. (*Author's collection*)

Side view of the 'Flyer', 1906. Shortly after its flight, the historic machine was blown over and wrecked by a sudden gust of wind. *(Colin J. Ashford Collection)*

production of carriages. A hip cradle for the operator, similar to that found in the gliders, enabled him to control the wing-warping and rudder operation. There was no throttle with which to regulate the engine, its function being taken instead by an on-and-off switch, a system that was to last until it was superseded by the far more 'sophisticated' aircraft designed for service in the First World War.

The new powered aircraft which had a span of 40 feet 4 inches (40 feet 2 inches according to some), a length of 21 feet or 20.37 feet and a wing area of 510 square feet, was too big and heavy to be launched by the method that had sufficed for the gliders (namely by manhandling to the top of a sand dune before being launched into wind so taking advantage of the gravitational pull). Hence the brothers had to come up with an alternative method. This consisted of the machine running under its own power along a 60 foot wooden rail – 'The Grand Central Junction Railroad'. It travelled along this on a pair of bicycle wheel hubs, one permanently set under the front of the machine, the other carried on a small wooden truck running along the rail supporting the rear of the aircraft. The machine was freed from this construction as soon as flying speed had been reached.

The point had now come for a move back to Kill Devil Hills. Once there, however, it seemed that the elements had conspired to frustrate their plans. Late October that year proved especially cold, the nights incredibly bitter while persistent storms restricted the time available for the brothers to hone their

A studio portrait of Wilbur at about the time of the brothers' success, which he always declared to have been achieved in equal measure with Orville. *(Author's collection)*

flying skills with the aid of No. 3 glider (No. 2 was not rated a particular loss when it was found to have become warped and unusable as a result of being stored in the camp kitchen).

Nor was that the end of their problems. When 'the whopper flying machine' was being readied for ground testing on 5 November 1903, every-thing seemed to go wrong. The magneto refused to emit a sufficiently 'fat' spark and as a result it proved impossible to coax the motor to run smoothly so that the uneven running damaged one of the tubular propeller shafts and both had to be removed. Sent back to Dayton the shafts were exchanged for a pair of heavier gauge, but this run of bad luck was compounded when the driving sprockets carrying the chains from the motor proved almost impossible to tighten.

By now the harsh weather, the frustrations and probably the realisation that if their efforts over the past several years were crowned with success they were about to be set apart from other men, all conspired to place the pair under a strain so severe that even the appearance of visitors – usually most welcome – taxed their natural gentlemanly manners. It is the period which marked the beginning of the unfounded belief that the brothers were soon to become habitually suspicious.

The appearance at the camp of Chanute for a six-day visit that lasted until 12 November contributed to their stress. They suspended some of their work on the 'whopper' and did their best to entertain him, all the time becoming increasingly depressed by his conversation which they saw as critical of their efforts; they were relieved when he finally left. Eight days later the repaired airscrew shafts appeared and the brothers were able to busy themselves fitting them (some sources assert that these were new ones of heavier gauge). Even

The later, improved Wright Type 'A' biplane design in flight over Huffman Prairie. *(Author's collection)*

their attempts to relax from the physical demands of the inhospitable surroundings centred around the powered flying machine. (Consciously seeking an antidote to their obsessive work, Orville took the determined step of studying languages.) But frustration was not far off and there was fresh trouble when it was discovered that one of the new propeller shafts had cracked. As a result the decision was taken to replace them with solid stock; the work was completed and the machine ready by 12 December.

The following day, a Monday, turned out to be beautiful but calm, with insufficient wind for a level take-off. The morning was spent repairing the machine's damaged tail, but when this was completed the pair decided on an attempt from the slope of Big Kill Devil Hill. They posted the agreed signal, a red flag, for the men of the Life Saving Station a mile away who were to act as assistants and witnesses, and before long the brothers were joined by John T. Daniels, Tom Beacham, Will S. Doug and 'Uncle Benny' O'Neal who helped drag the 750 lb machine to the hill half a mile away and up the 150 feet of its side. This took almost three-quarters of an hour so that it was 2.40 p.m. before the machine was set on its trolley and balanced on the track of the 'Junction Railroad', and the motor started – much to the discomfiture of a number of small boys who accompanied the men, the younger ones running off.

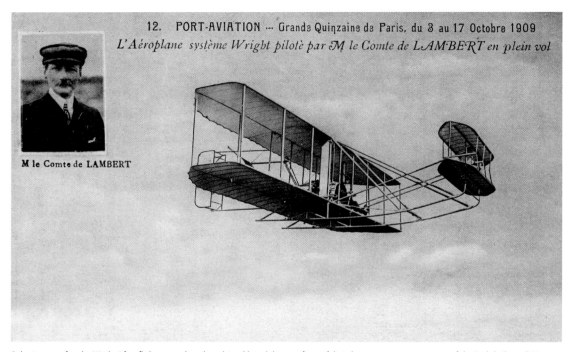

12.   PORT-AVIATION --- Grande Quinzaine de Paris, du 3 au 17 Octobre 1909
L'Aéroplane système Wright piloté par M le Comte de LAMBERT en plein vol

M le Comte de LAMBERT

Only six years after the Wrights' first flight postcards such as this publicised the use of one of their designs to attempt a crossing of the English Channel. Here, one piloted by le Comte de Lambert is pitted against Latham's Antoinette and Blériot's monoplane. *(Author's collection)*

While the motor was warming up, Orville and Wilbur drew a little apart and one tossed a coin to decide who should have the privilege of acting as pilot; Wilbur won the call. But when he took his place prone on the cradle that would control the movements of the machine and released the trolley clip, nothing happened – the weight of the machine was preventing it from opening and time was lost while this was adjusted. This done, the 'Flyer' then began to roll down the slope so suddenly that Orville, taken by surprise, failed to get a proper grip to steady it, losing his hold completely once the machine had travelled some 40 feet. Then, leaving the metal-faced monorail, the aircraft rose into the air with the nose pointing too sharply upwards, turned from the effect of a cross-wind and struck the ground, breaking some struts of the front rudder. This was a melancholy end to the Wrights' first attempt at powered flight, but one that seemingly left Wilbur not at all cast down; in a letter he wrote home the same evening he recorded: 'There is now no question of final success. . . . We anticipate no further trouble with landings.' Orville would later write of the same event: '. . . the method adopted for launching the machine was a safe and practicable one. On the whole, we are much pleased.'

Another contemporary artist's impression of a Wright Type 'A', which unfortunately shows the radius of the front booms to be too great and the elevators consequently set too high. *(Author's collection)*

It was to take two days before the damage to the machine was fully repaired, so that the brothers decided to schedule a further attempt for Thursday 17 December, this time from a level spot to take advantage of the 24 to 27 mph wind that was blowing. Again the signal was made to the proud, hard men of the Life Saving Station, to be answered by the eventual appearance of Adam D. Etheridge, John T. Daniels, Will S. Dough, with W.C. Brinkley, a lumber merchant from Manteo and young Jonny Moore, who lived with his widowed mother at Nags Head. They walked into camp before the Wrights were ready as the preparations were taking a little longer than before; Orville had taken it into his head to set up a camera on his tripod, focusing it on the point where the machine was expected to rise from its rail and into free flight. John Daniels was detailed to photograph as soon as the aeroplane began to rise.

His preparations complete, the party was quickly directed to assist in dragging the machine out of its shed and mounting it on the take-off rail, heavy work which they were happy to carry out, made harder by the bitter cold, the overnight rain lying in frozen puddles. Once the machine was mounted on its rail, the brothers started the engine by pulling on both airscrews, then they walked a little way off, leaving the motor running to warm up.

Wilbur and Orville too were feeling the freezing temperature, leaving the preparations from time to time to try and keep warm indoors for a short spell by holding their hands over the stove. One of the life-saving crew recalled that 'We couldn't help but notice how they held on to each other's hands, sort o' like two folks parting who weren't sure if they'd ever see each other again.'

This time it was Orville's turn to fly. First settling himself into the cradle, he pulled the release catch, allowing the machine to move forward into the gusting wind.

It started very slowly, so slowly in fact that Wilbur had no difficulty in running alongside to balance the machine until it lifted into the air at much the same spot as it had done a few days before when he had been in control. Someone looked at their watch. The time was exactly 10.03 a.m.

Once in the air, his brother found it difficult to maintain control of the machine, not only because of his lack of experience but also due to the force of the wind. Then, with a sudden and unexpected dart, the machine lost flying speed and struck the ground; it had flown a distance of some 120 feet from the point where Orville had released it 12 seconds earlier. Elated and confident, Orville crawled from his undignified position to receive the congratulations of his brother before the life-saving crew arrived to move the machine back to its starting point. From there three further flights would be attempted that day, the longest of which was 852 feet, covered in a time of 59 seconds. Like the previous flights, these were made at a negligible altitude since both men agreed that it was probably unsafe to rise too high under the prevailing conditions, despite the fact that the machine showed a greater control capacity than any of the gliders tested earlier. The flights that day had been of a distinctly undulating type, alternately scraping the ground before rising and then descending once more.

Those who had gathered to witness the historic events of that December morning were standing about discussing what they had seen with the biplane standing unattended a short distance off when an especially fierce gust took them all by surprise, at the same time beginning to turn the aircraft over. Everyone made a concerted dash in its direction, Wilbur, who was nearest, seizing the front, while Orville and John Daniels, nearer the tail, grabbed the struts at the back and attempted to prevent the machine being completely flung over.

All their best efforts proved in vain and the machine was turned on its back. Daniels, still retaining his grip, was taken with it and tossed head over heels inside what was rapidly being reduced to a jumble of chains, wires, bent chain guides and splintered timber along with a damaged motor; the man was badly bruised and knocked about for his pains.

Despite the knowledge that the machine which had that morning changed the course of history would never fly again, the brothers' elation was such that after lunch they walked the 4 miles to Kitty Hawk in order to send a telegram to Milton. The original contained a number of errors; it read: 'Bishop M. Wright, 7 Hawthorn St. Success four flights thursday morning all against twentyone mile wind started from Level with engine power alone average speed through air thirty one miles longest 57 seconds inform Press home Christmas. Orevelle Wright.' Perhaps the Western Union telegraph operator was overawed by the message he had to send; perhaps he did not believe it, but he certainly made several mistakes as this verbatim rendition shows!

The telegram arrived at 5.30 p.m. the same day and was taken upstairs to the bishop as he worked in his study. He had hardly had time to read it before his daughter Katherine came home from work and it was shown to her; she immediately set out again to telegraph the good news to brother Lorin who in turn did as his brothers had bidden and informed the press. The news was coldly received. This was to be typical.

Nevertheless a minority of newspapers did carry the story, however garbled. Here is an example taken from an English paper; the forward-looking *Daily Mail* devoted less than two column inches to the event which it reported at the bottom of a page in its issue of 19 December:

BALLOONLESS AIRSHIP

New York, Friday Dec. 18

Messrs. Wilbur and Orville Wright, of Ohio, yesterday successfully experimented with a flying machine at Kittyhawk, North Carolina. The machine has no balloon attachment, and derives its force from propellers worked by a small engine.

In the face of a wind blowing twenty-one miles an hour the machine flew three miles at the rate of eight miles an hour, and descended at a point selected in advance. The idea of the box-kite was used in the construction of the airship.

Despite the success that it brought the brothers, the Wright 'Flyer' of 1903 was little more than a test-rig with which to prove their theories; clearly, the next move would be to develop it into a reliable flying machine. The first phase of this was the evolution of the Flyer II completed in May 1904 and flown from the 90-acre Huffman Prairie, pasture owned by a friend some 8 miles east of Dayton.

Paul de Lesseps' Blériot monoplane restrained by helpers at Doncaster in 1910 as the motor is run at full throttle. *(The Flight Collection)*

Mlle Dutrieu in her Henry Farman biplane at Doncaster with M. Bau in the passenger seat, 1910. *(The Flight Collection)*

The dimensions of the Flyer II were similar to those of the prototype; it had the same control arrangements as well as a prone position for the operator but the camber was less and the engine more powerful, giving a force of some 16 hp. After a lengthy period devoted to adjustments and perfecting each element, this machine attained a total airborne time of 45 minutes spread between about one hundred starts that resulted in some eighty flights between 23 May and 9 December. The best flight lasted 5 minutes and 4 seconds and covered a distance of 2¾ miles. In May of the same year the brothers would introduce a system of assisted take-off using the energy of a falling weight to catapult the aircraft along its monorail.

This system was to prove of special value during launchings from wet grass and during the demonstrations they were soon to give, spectators considering it something of a privilege to be allowed to haul the heavy weight to the top of the derrick from where it fell. Attached to a rope running under the aircraft to its nose, the fall of the weight could be triggered by the pilot so that the machine shot forward until its nose was raised, thus withdrawing the pin which attached the rope to the tow-bar and freeing the aircraft which was catapulted into a shallow climb. This system was first used on 7 December and had the advantage of making take-offs independent of the strength of the wind as well as its direction. Further, although this method of launching was of value since it made unnecessary the use of small, unprepared fields, the Wright machine was perfectly capable of taking off without its aid. The necessity of flying from small fields had been one reason for the retention of skids rather than the adoption of wheels, this later causing comment from uninformed critics who were also surprised to note that propeller speeds less than that of the engine were achieved by means of the simple gearing.

Nevertheless, despite the many small advances that the stay at Huffman Prairie was to see, there was also the problem of attempting not to overfly other property, something that was especially difficult to avoid if a tight turn were attempted, when the machine had a tendency to stall, and it was not until the following year that the problem was overcome with the assistance of Flyer III. This machine was quite different from the original 'Flyer', although it resembled it; the elevator was further forward and the rudder further back than had previously been the case, while the camber of the 4 foot 6 inch wings was increased. In side elevation the Model III was immediately identifiable from the upward slope of the upper rear booms.

It was 1905 and the Wrights were still at Huffman Prairie, a field they were to continue to use between 23 June and 16 October. They were now achieving speeds of 35 mph, a small improvement on that of the 1904 Flyer II which had been broken up and destroyed.

Much of the work of 1904 was devoted to finding a solution to the problem of the stalling associated with tight turns. Some forty flights with a total time of three hours were expended to this end, but it was not until September that they finally diagnosed the problem as due to the lower wings slowing and failing to give adequate lift on the inside of a turn. Once this was appreciated, it immediately became clear that a simple cure lay in putting the nose down and

In Western Europe, among the most significant events of 1910 was that of 2 June when the Hon. C.S. Rolls, flying a Wright biplane, crossed the English Channel in a single flight in both directions in one day without landing. This is the memorial to the event at Dover, his departure and return point. It is the work of Lady Scott, wife of Capt. R.F. Scott the Antarctic explorer. *(Author)*

so making good the lost speed. It was also at this time that Wilbur and Orville took the serious decision that the time had now come to disconnect the linkage that joined the wing-warping to the rudder controls, thus leaving the two systems capable of independent operation.

Only two years after their first tentative steps with a powered aircraft on the Kill Devil Hills, the two bicycle-shop owners from Dayton had solved the problem that had defeated mankind down the ages. They had at their command a flying machine, the first practicable example of its kind in history, that was capable of staying airborne for 38 minutes 3 seconds, the best time that year, and of covering a distance of more than 24 miles in the process.

At first it might seem strange that between mid-October 1905 and 6 May 1908 neither Wilbur nor Orville left the ground. In part this was due to Wilbur's concern that overexposure of their invention would place its results in too public a light, where they could simply be stolen by even a casual observer equipped with only minimal know-how.

Not that this meant that the brothers lived the lives of recluses, although they did take the precaution of confining their social circle to those whom they could trust. Nor did it mean that they idled away two and a half years of their lives adding nothing to the scientific advances they had created for their generation; in fact, they spent their time productively, putting their knowledge to work in the development of a number of improved derivatives of the 'Flyer' and turning their attention to similar work on the engines.

908 glider is manhandled by a team of three to its take-off point. *(Courtesy of Special Collections and Archives, Wright State University, Ohio)*

ider, which represents
'rights' post-powered
trials, in 'full flight' as it
have been described at
me. The peculiar
jement of the
gular rudder forward of
ilplane is of interest.
view the pilot is said
Orville. *(Author's
tion)*

Severe gusts of wind have upset the 1908 glider here with Orville in the pilot's position. Helpers rush forward. *(Author's collection)*

The same incident a few moments later. The glider settles down and is held to give Orville a chance to escape since it is in danger of falling backwards. *(Courtesy of Special Collections and Archives, Wright State University, Ohio)*

Foremost among the new aeroplanes was the model soon to be designated the Wright Type 'A'. The general configuration of this machine, while clearly based on the original historic version, could now accommodate two persons, no longer prone as the first lone operative had been, but sitting upright on adjacent seats. This modification was another significant advance since it eventually allowed the brothers to take on flights various people from all walks of life. These early passengers included their father Bishop Milton Wright; Madam Hart O. Berg, the first lady to fly and wife of the manager of Flint European's operations who hoped to become their agent; their sister Katherine, watched by Queen Victoria's eldest son, the then King Edward VII; Alfonso XIII, King of Spain; Griffith Brewer, later to become their European sales manager; and a number of other men who would in time make their own contributions to the new world of aeronautics. All these and more were taken aloft without charge in a machine that boasted dimensions which make interesting comparison with the first 'Flyer'. The new derivative had a wingspan of 41 feet, a length of 31 feet and a speed capability that could rise to a maximum of 40 mph driven by a 30/40-hp motor.

The 1908 glider flies out over the wastes of sand, allegedly with Ogilvie at the controls; three onlookers are seen in the foreground. *(Author's collection)*

Although of poor quality, this photograph is of interest since it shows part of the line of tented hangars at Bournemouth in 1910. From left to right: COLMORE RADLEY, whose Blériot monoplane is attracting interest in the foreground; RAWLINSON, holder of the next RAeC certificate after Rolls and who was to break an ankle on the day of the other's death; he would later take charge of London's gun defences in the First Word War; he flew a Farman; DREXEL JONES, an American entrant flying a Blériot monoplane; and GRACE, flying a Short. Among the sixteen other entrants and their aircraft were: the Hon. A. Boyle, flying an Avis; Wagner with a Hanriot; Morane bringing his Blériot; Alec Ogilvie and Rolls both in Wrights; Dickson, Grahame White, Audemans (a Belgian) and Cockburn each with a Farman; Barnes flying a Humber; Cody with a machine of his own design; and Christiaes (aircraft type not known). *(Author's collection)*

As is the way in all developing sciences, not all these Type 'A' machines were identical; although they are generally regarded as products of 1908, a number were in fact constructed the previous year. Some differed in detail from the models which would soon be manufactured under licence not only at home, but also in Great Britain, France and Germany. But perhaps the greatest deviation from any attempt to produce a 'standard' machine was a 'Flyer' for the United States government. It was constructed only after two official refusals, the first the result of the erroneous belief on the part of the authorities that the Wrights were seeking financial backing for their work, the second when a demonstration was blighted by the death of Lieutenant Selfridge (see below, p. 145).

The Type 'A', which was never described as such except retrospectively, now came to be regarded as the standard form of the Wright model for 1908–9. Indeed, Orville believed that every member of the exhibition team about to be

French-built Wright biplane being towed on to the flying field a few days before his death. *(The Flight Collection)*

Wright machine photographed over the spot where he was to perish on the following day. *(Author's collection)*

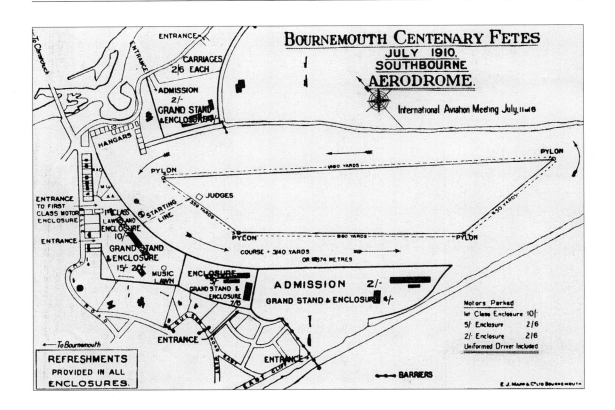

formed should fly this type. Team members took turns to display this lone
machine, representative of the type as a whole, not as is the modern manner,
each man giving formation displays on a different type.

Alas this idea was killed off almost immediately when 21-year-old Walter
Brookins destroyed the model in a crash. Orville then ordered preparation of
the even more up-to-date Wright Type 'B'. However, Ralph Johnstone, whose
turn it now was, had limited experience of flying a machine with a wheeled
undercarriage, lost control, and rolled into a line of parked automobiles.

There was more trouble ahead. At the Wisconsin State Fair display, Arch
Hoxley had an accident that proved fatal when he completely lost control
during a low pass and simply 'fell out of the sky', killing himself and a number
of spectators.

Understandably, this catalogue of accidents troubled the Wrights, and the
two latest pilots to entertain the crowd with a little blood received a sharp
letter from Wilbur, who stressed that wild flying would bring them no credit.
However, the warning seemed to fall on deaf ears; the irresponsible flying – and

Colmore Radley's Blériot monoplane excited much interest in being powered, not with an Anzani motor as was the machine used for Blériot's Channel crossing the year before, but with an 80-hp E.N.V. water-cooled motor (to judge from the rectangular radiator). *(Bournemouth Library Services)*

The Rolls-Royce monogram. It was originally red, but remains in black to this day as a sign of mourning for Royce's partner, Charlie Rolls.

with it the accidents – continued, reaching a climax at Denver in November when Johnstone was killed. After this latest piece of bad news, at the end of his business trip to Germany Orville returned home thoroughly depressed, due in part to the tale going the rounds that the fatalities were caused by a built-in design feature that made the type dangerous to fly. This was no way to encourage business, and in November 1911 the only sensible course was taken and the display team disbanded.

Nor were troubles of this kind the only ones to haunt the brothers. Law suits were being conducted by the pair against those whom they believed were stealing their patents, while others had clearly done just that and were seeking compensation from the brothers in the form of handsome damages, alleging that the thieves were in fact the Wrights.

FOUR

MARKETS

When [Victor Loughead] learned at first-hand from half a dozen different persons who had been eye-witnesses of the flight . . . he skipped out without ever even seeing the machine!

Orville Wright, 1911

Human, mechanical flight was, of course, impossible. No less an authority than Isaac Newton had seemed to prove this in 1687, nor had anyone gainsaid him during the intervening years when he had declared that the air was made up of minute independent particles and that it was thus incapable of supporting a body suspended in it. Small wonder, then, that there existed a vast body of opinion even some two hundred and fifty years later, which still accepted this fallacy as gospel and tended to believe that the Wrights were the most brazen confidence tricksters of all time.

Nor were their detractors, eager for endorsement of their cynicism, without facts to 'support' their disbelief. Had not the claims to have flown been made as long ago as 1903, and now, in 1908, little or nothing had been heard of the brothers or their claims. This was certainly true; Wilbur and Orville had last been known to have flown on 16 October in the year of their claim. Had they now withdrawn from the glare of publicity in order to escape ridicule?

The fact is that, as Wilbur had stated, the salient points of their invention were abundantly clear to even the most casual observer. Hence, in order to protect the fruits of their meticulous scientific endeavours, the pair deemed it best not to place too much emphasis on public display too often, and allowed what seemed an astonishing 'interregnum' to intervene in order to safeguard their rights. This period was later remembered and explained by assertions that the brothers were secretive to the point of paranoia.

A new method of take-off was in fact introduced in 1906 and consisted of a derrick to the apex of which an 1,764-lb-weight was hauled and then allowed to drop via a rope running over pulleys, shooting the machine forward along its

An unidentified Wright Type 'A' showing the small rudders between the forward horizontal surfaces and the straighter line of the booms than on the prototypes. *(Author's collection)*

Judging by the number of uniformed figures and the early type of aircraft, this photograph seems to show military trials of a Wright machine, the launching derrick and its equipment dominating the foreground. (*Author's collection*)

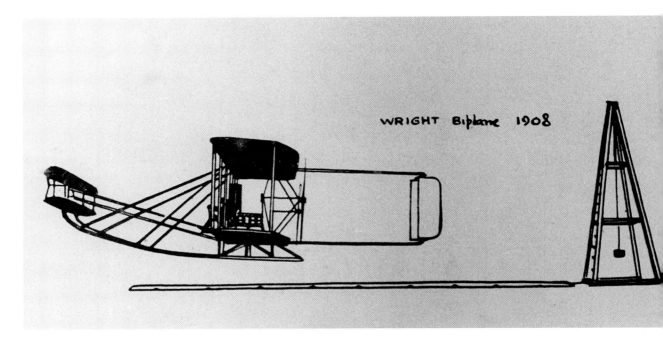

A near-contemporary drawing showing the basic Wright launching system. *(Courtesy Jane's Information Group)*

metal-sheathed rail; when the pilot raised the nose of the machine, the rope was released and fell harmlessly away. It is on record that soon it was considered a privilege for volunteers to haul the weight into position during the preparations for a flight. Operations beginning with a launch by this method were to prove more reliable than from grass if this was wet, although under dry conditions the 'Flyers' could and did operate without the derrick's assistance, using engine power alone.

Clearly, it was now time for the Wrights to begin flying once more, introducing their aircraft to potential customers in Europe following an agreement with a French company, permitting it to build their machines only after lengthy negotiations. The year was 1908; the two men began preparing for their sales tour with some twenty practice flights using the old Flyer III, once again operating from Kill Devil Hills. This time Wilbur departed alone as Orville was still to make a complete recovery from injuries sustained in the crash that had killed Lieutenant Selfridge.

As it turned out, a machine of the Type 'A' pattern was already in France waiting, crated for collection at Le Havre having been dispatched the previous year. The plan was to assemble it after Wilbur's arrival, in the car factory owned by Léon Bollée. Bollée was an enthusiastic, ebullient, rotund, bustling,

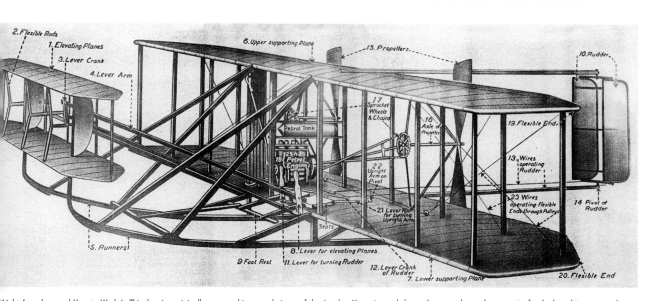

...right Aeroplane and How to Work It. This drawing originally appeared in an early issue of the *London Magazine* and shows the catapult attachment point for the launching gear — the ...t horizontal member forward of the footrest between the pair of front runners. *(Author's collection)*

...w an early Wright biplane, this is one of several photographs taken of the second longest flight of the 1905 season. It took place on 4 October and lasted for 33⅓ minutes, covering ...niles. *(Author's collection)*

Servicing a Wright biplane. This photograph shows the substantial control members, fuel tank and radiator. The wheeled vehicle in the foreground is a trolley to assist in moving the machine into position on the launching rail. *(The Flight Collection)*

bearded, stocky man who, true to his promise to find a suitable flying area for Wilbur, procured the use of fields some 5 miles south of Le Mans. It was from there that the first public flight in France was made, consisting of no more than two graceful turns before landing after 105 seconds. Other flights would last as long as 8 minutes.

Later, a move was made to the great oval racecourse at Hunaudières, but hardly had reassembly work commenced at the new venue than an accident befell Wilbur when on 4 July, near-boiling water escaping from a broken rubber connection to the radiator scalded his left arm. The ensuing delay caused a number of sceptics to assert that here was evidence that flight had never been achieved in America, with some newspaper headlines proclaiming 'Le Bluff Continue'.

Meanwhile a hut was constructed at Hunaudières and a launching derrick erected so that, his arm barely healed, Wilbur was able to make his first flight from the continent of Europe on 8 August. He was watched by an audience not only gathered from the neighbouring countryside but that included representatives of the press and the Aero Club de France.

The graceful banks and turns that the machine performed on that memorable day astonished the assembled onlookers. Louis Blériot, who would himself enter the history books with his cross-Channel flight in July the following year, summed up the excitement: 'A new era in mechanical flight has commenced. . . . It is marvellous.' No less impressive was the spectacle of Wilbur's quiet confidence. So certain was he of his machine's performance that he deemed any practice flights unnecessary, with the result that the now repentant French press reacted similarly, some quoting Blériot and similar accolades.

A visitor to the camp at Hunaudières provides an interesting glimpse into this world. He tells how at first he could see no sign of the American. Only later did he learn that part of the hangar had been partitioned off to form a living room for Wilbur and that it contained a couple of chairs and a table where he could have his meals in some privacy and, since he was in the habit of sleeping every night near to the machine, even a bed.

The visitor's first sight of 'the great Wilbur' revealed a slim, erect figure who spoke slowly, quietly and deliberately, never under any circumstances in a hurry. He related how once, when assured by a mechanic that an adjustment had been carried out, and without giving any indication that he doubted the man, Wilbur climbed down from his seat to satisfy himself that the work had indeed been properly executed.

The flying display was equally impressive, the 'Flyer' being taken up to a height of some 300 feet, seeming to hover for a moment, and then swooping down to 200 feet before making a smooth landing in front of its shed. For a few seconds the crowd was so awed that a silence greeted the landing, to be broken by a great outburst of cheering and applause.

Wherever he went now, Wilbur earned fresh popularity from the once censorious press reporters, in part the result of his habit of treating them with courtesy and always being prepared to answer their questions in full. Typical of this new-found relationship was the appearance of a special cover of *Le Petit Journal*, in later years accounted a collector's item, while fresh excitement broke out in December. That month during a flight the engine of the machine was deliberately shut down, the aircraft gliding to the ground in unaccustomed silence. The noiseless performance must have seemed profound as the Wright motors soon earned a reputation for their quiet functioning, the main noise that of the rattle of the chains in their tubular guides driving the airscrews. Two days after the incident with the motor, Wilbur claimed the headlines again with a flight of 54 minutes 53.4 seconds duration.

This triumph was followed by an aerial journey of only a little less than two and a half hours, all the more remarkable in view of the weather's deterioration. Seeking warmer climes for their guest Tissandier, an admired balloonist who subsequently learned to pilot a heavier-than-air craft, Wilbur suggested a move to Pau on the edge of the Pyrenees, and it was here that he was joined by Orville and their sister Katherine.

The three had much to discuss. Orville had recently received a song composed in honour of the brothers by Mrs Mary E. Knostman who had autographed the gifted sheet which featured on its front an artist's impression in colour of a Wright biplane flying high over the Californian countryside. Published by a local firm, Reisbach & Knostman of 109 Zeigler, Dayton, it confirmed the brothers' prestige at home. Further token of the Wrights' popularity lay in the fact that Katherine was about to 'learn' from certain newspapers that she constantly made helpful suggestions to her

The Wright brothers' gifted sister Katherine, seen here on the occasion of her graduation from Oberlin College in 1898. (*Author's collection*)

brothers on the finer points of aircraft design, regularly solved mathematical problems that were beyond them and quietly financed their experiments! This was nothing more than unfounded newspaper allegations, of course, although there is no doubt that she was an extraordinarily intelligent and gifted young woman.

In acknowledgement of the fact that they were the first celebrities of the new century, the press still followed the two men wherever they went. Now it was Orville who dealt with the questions, Wilbur merely adding a few points where he thought necessary, but there was no real change in the Wright attitude to interviews – Orville dealt with them in the same way as Wilbur had done, without impatience, haste or irritation.

But the spectacle and press attention was only one side of their operation; the purpose of their globe-trotting was the acquisition of business and at the close of the period agreements had been finalised for the manufacture of Wright aircraft in the key industrial countries of Europe – France, Germany and Great

Advertisement featuring the Herring-Curtiss biplane. *(Courtesy John W.R. Taylor)*

A later Wright biplane incorporating such refinements as a seat for the pilot. (*Author's collection*)

Britain. In Britain, manufacture was entrusted to Shorts, but it was in a Wright machine constructed by the Compagnie Générale de Navigation Aérienne, usually referred to as the French-Wright Company and earlier formed from the Lazare Weillers syndicate, that the first Englishman died in a flying accident. Charlie Rolls was killed at the Bournemouth meeting of 1910 when the tail unit, modified with an additional surface supported on flimsy outriggers, broke away during the spot landing competition of 12 July. He had gained his first air experience at Le Mans during the previous October with Wilbur piloting, Rolls later commenting: 'The power of flight is as a gift from the Creator, the greatest treasure yet given to man.' It was another Wright customer, Frank McClean, who was later to earn notoriety by flying under all the Thames bridges between the Tower and Westminster, although he used a Short S.33 pusher floatplane for this escapade, not a Wright.

But for the Wrights, now in Italy, it was time to turn their thoughts homeward and the journey was begun, taking in Paris and then London en route. Fêted wherever they went, the English capital proved no exception, the brothers being awarded gold medals by the Aeronautical Society and the Aero Club (neither yet styled 'Royal') before at last making the Atlantic crossing, finally to arrive home in May.

Back in the familiar surroundings of Dayton, it immediately became clear that there was to be no slipping into the routine to which they had become accustomed as 'ordinary folk'. Instead, they had to cope with two-day welcoming ceremonials, a ten-minute cacophony from every works siren and hooter in the area, and a parade of bands playing martial music which escorted their open carriage through the streets. This was followed by another round of celebrations in the afternoon of 17 June, until finally the two men were able to escape back to the old bicycle shop. Even this respite was to be short-lived since they were expected to attend a firework display in their honour that evening.

The next day brought no let-up. There were further medals to be received at several ceremonies, with their father, Bishop Milton Wright, now in attendance. Octave Chanute summed up the brothers' probable feelings: 'You must be pretty well satiated with glory.' He was right. It was with relief that Wilbur and Orville slipped away from the last of the cloying ceremonials as soon as they decently could. At heart they were still the same, unchanged local men who had kept a bicycle repair business in the town. The next day they had a train to catch that would take them to Washington; soon they would be fully committed to the aircraft trials on behalf of the US Army at Fort Meyer.

True to their policy of meticulous attention to detail, leaving nothing to chance, it was not until 29 June that the brothers settled upon the aircraft they were to use. It lay tuned and ready, but the delay suddenly triggered a shift in public attitude and the heroes who had been fêted but a short while since, suddenly became the targets of vilification. To this was added mortification when Orville, who was to carry out all the flying, broke a landing skid on the second day and did more serious damage a few days later, running the machine into a tree.

...ss 'F' flying boat with short-span wings, inter-gap ailerons and fabric 'curtains' between the inner strut bays to act as an 'anti-skid' device. With the passage of time, the Glen Curtiss ...ation tended to specialise in flying boats. *(Bruce Robertson Collection)*

A Wright Type 'A' in flight. Those models produced under licence in Europe were powered by a suitable motor of the customer's choice. *(Author's collection)*

Events such as these heralded a period of change which was to render the happy days when they were no more than ambitious shopkeepers, a distant memory. They both recalled Wilbur's wise comment of three years earlier, that their invention could too easily be copied. And it now became clear that this was exactly what was happening; it was not long before the pair became embroiled in seemingly endless litigation in an attempt to protect their patents. Not only right and proper, that they chose this course was hardly surprising. Resorting to action in the courts was normal for them and something with which they had been familiar as younger men, Milton having resorted to litigation on numerous occasions to settle disputes in the Church.

Although there were many court cases involving the brothers, in all of these it was Wilbur who took the lead in the defence, quickly becoming almost permanently active in protecting his and his brother's rights. Perhaps the best-known and most typical instance was the action against the Glen Curtiss organisation, now operating in a business association with Augustus Herring. The point at issue centred on a machine known as the 'Golden Flier' which that organisation had constructed. The machine's controls included mid-wing ailerons and the Wrights argued that these were an infringement of their own

A frequent choice of alternative power-plant in England was this 30-hp Green engine. *(Author's collection)*

patent. When news that a suit had been filed in New York by Wilbur reached Orville, then in Berlin with his sister, he immediately wrote to his brother suggesting that a public declaration be issued to the effect that legal proceedings would be taken against all suspected infringements of Wright patents. But it was not until January 1910 that a circuit court issued an injunction restraining the Herring-Curtiss Company from, among other activities, 'the manufacture of flying machines' with the result that by early April the organisation was forced to file for bankruptcy.

However, this was not the end of the matter. Herring claimed that the bankruptcy declaration was no more than a ploy to get rid of him and, as a result, this suit was rejected in December, and the earlier injunction was withdrawn by the Appeals Court. But argument and counter-argument continued and it was to be a further four years before the dispute was finally

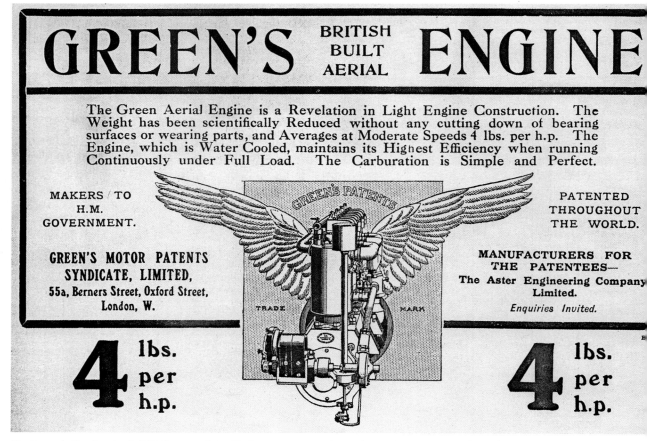

Advertisement for Green's engines in 1909. These were designed by the pioneer aero-motor designer Gustavias Green. Born in 1864 he was thirty-two when he moved to Bexhill-on-Sea, Sussex, where he opened a cycle shop (like the Wrights and Curtiss) at 5 Western Road, moving this business to 49 Reginald Road in 1902. He died on 29 December 1964, some three months short of his hundredth birthday. (*Author's collection*)

laid to rest, and even then it was subject to an appeal. By then, however, the Wright family had on its hands a contest of even greater importance, and one which no court could settle.

Throughout this period both of the Wrights had been occupied by the business they had been instrumental in creating, despite allegations to the contrary by some who, sadly, included Chanute. At seventy-eight Chanute was even nearer to death than anyone imagined, albeit he was busy fabricating rumours to the contrary. But in addition to discharging the brothers' commercial responsibilities, Wilbur continued to apply his fine analytical mind, which had contributed so much to the understanding of aerodynamics and engineering, to championing his rights and those of his brother. The family could not fail to notice the increasing frequency with which, looking drawn and haggard, he returned from visits to their lawyer.

It therefore came as no surprise when Wilbur, away from home on a visit to Boston, was suddenly taken ill in April 1912. He had spent the preceding four months dealing simultaneously with four law suits, but it was a meal of shellfish that was blamed rather than exhaustion, particularly as, arriving home some two weeks later, he claimed to feel better. So it was with lightened hearts that Milton and his three unmarried children enjoyed a picnic the same afternoon. Alas, Wilbur complained of feeling ill when they returned home, the doctor who was called diagnosing malaria. The following morning, the patient felt no worse but his temperature had risen. But Wilbur ignored his symptoms and travelled to Huffman Prairie, later writing an uncharacteristic letter to an employee, couched in unnecessarily vehement terms.

Four days later he was clearly worse. The doctor was again summoned, this time revising his opinion. The malady was in fact typhoid, the same fever from which Orville had recovered sixteen years before. Wilbur took no comfort from this and two days later, conscious that he was dying, dictated his will to his secretary. Although the prognosis of the doctor who had treated Orville was sought, there was no improvement, the patient's digestion and spleen were failing and he died on 30 May 1912.

ples of several types of Green-designed aero-motors developed just before the designer's retirement. The one in the immediate foreground is the 300-hp motor. (*Author's collection*)

A 'production type' Wright biplane in flight, showing the prominent radiator offset to starboard and the refinement of a seat for the pilot. *(Author's collection)*

After Wilbur's death, Orville Wright had to shoulder the entire responsibility for the business empire he and his brother had created. Orville lived long enough to see the flying machine develop beyond the imaginings of either brother. *(The Flight Collection)*

His passing took on something of the aura of a hero's death in the hour of victory. Those who had known him, and indeed the civilised world as a whole, reacted fittingly; during the funeral two days later, traffic drew into the kerb, streetcars (trams) stopped and the telephone switchboard fell silent. He left $289,298.40, the main beneficiaries being members of the family.

As their father would record, it was Orville and Katherine who experienced the sharpest pangs of loss. Ironically, twelve days later they had to attend the funerals of a pair who had been killed flying the new Wright C-1, but afterwards they were able to busy themselves with less distressing matters, Orville with his work and Katherine in anticipation of the regular visit to Europe which they would make in early February the following year.

Earlier there had been another catastrophy that had to be faced, this time a climatic one which took the form of floods that inundated the area following the collapse of a dam in March. Then the main anxiety had been for Bishop Milton and, once he was pronounced safe, attention was turned to the depth of water which caught Orville and his sister away from home and unable to return. They were forced to take refuge at the house of a friend, Orville all the time worried by the thought of the potential destruction of the Wright papers which recorded the brothers' preparations for their historic flight ten years earlier. The papers were kept on the second floor of the bicycle shop, but the irreplaceable photographs were in an old shed at the back of the house, so that their loss seemed certain since the water was already reported to be some 12 feet deep in places. But in the event both collections survived; only a few of the glass negatives had started to peel as a result of the water. This damage is still visible, particularly on some pictures showing Wilbur at the controls of the 'Flyer' which were slightly spoiled during the abortive attempt to fly on 14 December 1903. How close they came to destruction is evident from the wrinkled surface, particularly at the bottom of the picture.

Thankfully, another survivor of the 1913 Dayton floods was found to be the remains of the 1903 'Flyer'. Covered with yellowish mud, the parts remained intact in the packing cases into which they had been placed, with little thought as to their historical value, before being stacked in the shed behind the bicycle shop. Perhaps at some later date Orville would breathe a private sigh of relief when the value of the contents became clear. The 1903 'Flyer' survived not only water, but also fire. A blaze fed by the fractured gas mains of the town had swept through its streets, but almost miraculously had burnt itself out short of the bicycle shop in West Third Street. He did not open the cases. Why do so?

The brothers had always been more concerned with the future than the past. In this particular instance they had been wrong.

Just over a year later there were to be losses greater than material ones. The numbers of dead from the fighting in the First World War exceeded anything previously recorded, a cataclysm into which, in 1917, even the United States was drawn. One of the less obvious effects of the war was that every civilised branch of human endeavour suffered as a result of its outbreak, a material casualty in France being plans to erect a monument to Wilbur Wright, a project which was stalled until 1920.

The day scheduled for the unveiling was Saturday 17 July and the place, appropriately enough, Le Mans; it was here that Wilbur had astonished sceptical audiences eleven summers previously. Now the town was dominated by a huge marble sculpture by Landovski representing mankind's struggle to conquer the air, on its base figures in bas-relief representing Wilbur and Orville Wright with one of Wilbur's car-manufacturer friends, Léon Bollée, described as 'the Frenchman who collaborated in the dangerous experiments'. During the ceremonies modern aircraft circled overhead and among the wreaths were ones from the Wrights' home state of Ohio and the Aero Club of America.

Not unnaturally, the dedication of a monument to the memory of a man whom France had so recently taken to its heart attracted a number of official representatives. These included the French Air Minister, M. Flaudin; the former United States' Ambassador to Paris, Myron Herrick and the current ambassador, Admiral Maginder; General Dumesnil, representing the government; and le Compt Henri de la Vaulx. Interestingly, this monument pre-dated by some seven years the one eventually authorised by the US Congress. Originally known by its full title as the Wright Brothers National Memorial, it eventually came to be known more briefly as the Wright Memorial. It consisted of the 425-acre site covering the area where the world's first four flights had taken place, its centre dominated by a grey granite shaft, 60 feet high, erected on the crest of the highest of the Kill Devil Hills.

But while nations saluted the two men foremost in changing the world and dedicated their memory to posterity, it was argued that the Wright brothers left behind their own memorial in the number of varying aircraft types they had designed. Of these, the majority evolved naturally out of the basic Wright biplane that had astonished the world on the bitterly cold December day in 1903. Then, for a brief space of some 12 seconds, the brothers had achieved manned, controlled, powered flight. Nor was their success the fortuitous result of blundering about in the dark, as was the case with some of their

The US Signal Corps Aviation School at Augusta, Georgia, photographed from a Wright biplane flying an early type of 'Old Glory' from a strut. The photograph shows another machine of possibly the same type and a pair of canvas hangars in 1912, by which time the miracle of man's controlled flight was near to acceptance. *(Bruce Robertson Collection)*

competitors. They appreciated the extent of the problems involved and adhered to a process of careful scientific analysis, allying the results to practical experiments with courage, conviction and sheer doggedness. The outcome, the strange-looking kite-like contraption that was the world's first true powered flying machine, had conquered a world that had eluded solution by experimenters, and before them thinkers, even though many had unknowingly come close to triumph during earlier ages.

The first practical aeroplane that was anything more than a test-rig has therefore to be the model known retrospectively as the Wright Type 'A'. That designation applied to all the first perfected variants of the basic design, including those which had been built in 1907 but first flown in the following year and those produced later. This type was to be constructed at Dayton until as late as 1910, five years after the construction of the 'Flyer III', which it resembled. Inherently unstable, it was manufactured in America as well as in France, Germany and Great Britain. It had a wingspan of 41 feet, and a length of 31 feet. Its wing chord measured 6 feet 6 inches with a wing area of 510 square feet. Powered by a 40-hp Wright motor, it weighed 800 lb. The Type 'A' was capable of a maximum speed of 35 to 40 mph. Used for instruction, many of these were controlled by a lever activating the elevator to the right and left of the pilot's seat, with a single wing-warping control between the seats where it was handy for both instructor and pupil.

This arrangement was also used on the 1910 Type 'B', 'The headless Wright' machines used for instruction. However, its construction marked a radical departure from the earlier models, perhaps the chief modification being that the foreplanes supported on the previously extended booms were discarded, their lower parts now extended to prevent nosing over in a rough landing but carrying two comparatively small triangular fabric panels to increase the keel area. The rudder was carried on a rear outrigger considerably smaller than the previous type with a span of 38 feet, an area of 500 square feet and a length of 30 feet. The 40-hp Wright motor was retained.

When it was introduced in 1913, the Type 'C' was immediately declared 'obsolete', in part no doubt due to its having a clear relationship to the previous variant, even retaining the same dimensions. However, the engine was a 30 to 38-hp Wright, which made possible a maximum speed of 44 mph. Its weight was 1,380 lb. Interestingly, although US versions kept the peculiar Wright system of flying controls, some of those produced in Europe were fitted with control columns and rudder pedals. Type 'C' is also remembered for being dangerously tail-heavy, gaining dubious fame from the fact that the US Army purchased six, five of which were instrumental in killing six men. Allegedly, this was due to the fact that the rear elevator was insufficiently large and so incapable of correcting any over-rapid loss of height.

Matters did not improve with the introduction of the Type 'C-H'. A floatplane, this was immediately dubbed 'a clumsy Type "C" fitted with a 240 lb three-step pontoon', doubtless because its wings were similar in span to those of the earlier type. It was 29 feet 9 inches long. All-up weight was 1,610 lb while the motor was a 60-hp Wright which gave a quoted speed of 50 mph.

The Type 'C-1' was already in existence at the time of Wilbur's death in 1912; indeed, it was to pay their respects to two men killed flying this type that Orville and Katherine found themselves making the journey to Maryland to attend their funerals. Currently described as a 'new type', it had crashed as the

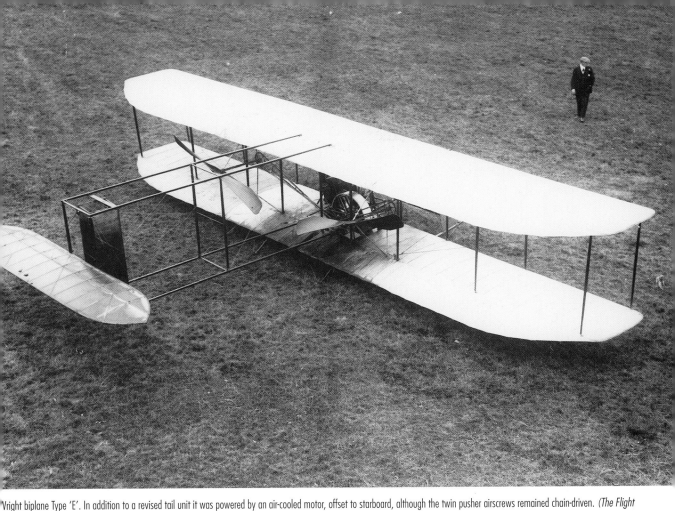

Wright biplane Type 'E'. In addition to a revised tail unit it was powered by an air-cooled motor, offset to starboard, although the twin pusher airscrews remained chain-driven. *(The Flight*
ction)

result of stalling when pulled up sharply to commence a climb to a pre-set altitude as part of a series of tests carried out to decide whether the type should be purchased for the US Army.

Few details have emerged of the Type 'E' except that it was a single-seater which, in October 1913, was experimentally fitted with an early automatic pilot. Its span was 32 feet.

The Wright Type 'EX' was a smaller version of the Type 'B', the best known form being that used for a pioneering step into aero-advertising. Specially modified and inscribed vertically with the name of the soft drink it trumpeted, 'Vin Fiz', on the vertical tail, it was used for the celebrated flight made in stages from Long Island to Long Beach in 1913.

With a wingspan 10 feet greater than that of the Type 'E', the 42-foot Type 'F' was significant in being the variant in whose design the bold step was taken of providing a closed, conventional fuselage for the occupants, together with a tail

Dunne's D.8 biplane. On 20 August 1913 it flew over Paris in connection with the Aero Show of that year. *(Bruce Robertson Collection)*

unit of the pattern that was soon to become the norm, and a wheeled undercarriage. However, it still retained the twin, pusher, chain-driven propellers of the original 'Flyer'. Intended for military use (see Chapter Eight), it had a length of 29 feet 6 inches and when loaded tipped the scale at 2,100 lb. It could attain a maximum speed of 60 mph and was powered by a 90-hp Austro-Daimler motor.

It was as late as 1914 that a Wright Type 'G', also known as the 'Aerobat', was purchased by the US Navy in the service of which it was numbered AH-19. But this floatplane was quickly rejected following tests which revealed its poor performance. It was followed by one of the least-known Wright machines, the Type 'HS', a model which was among the fastest, capable of a maximum speed of 70 mph. It had a wingspan of 32 feet and a length of 29 feet 6 inches. With a wing area of 350 square feet, it weighed 1,000 lb.

A reorganised Wright company operating from the autumn of 1915 found itself facing problems resulting from the lack of development potential inherent in the original design. To address this, two new variants appeared which bore little resemblance to their antecedents. These were to be known as Type 'K' and Type 'L', both of which featured a conventional fuselage with tractor propellers. The first was a new floatplane which, however, retained the old wing-warping system; the latter was similar. Neither was commercially successful.

The ultimate Wright type indicated a determined effort to break free from earlier design constraints, now considered archaic. In this it was only partially successful, although its designation of Type 'R' at least acknowledged the popularity of air racing in 1910. The 'Baby Wright', or 'Roadster' as it was known, had been conceived as a specialist entrant into the Gordon Bennet contest of that year. (James Gordon Bennett, the philanthropic editor of the *New York Herald* gave away vast sums of money promoting many branches of sport.) It retained the chain-driven pusher propellers of old, but incorporated such innovations as shortened skids, reminiscent of the Model 'B', and a four-wheel (two pairs of side-by-side wheels) undercarriage. Capable of a speed of 50 mph with the aid of an eight-cylinder 50/60-hp motor, its span was a mere 21 feet.

A special version of the even smaller model, popularly known as the 'Baby Grand', was generally regarded as the personal 'mount' of Orville Wright. Its modest size apart, it was distinguished by such details as a six-wheel undercarriage which was similar to that of the earlier machine but with the addition of a single wheel on the front of each landing skid. Small wonder that it attracted plenty of attention when Orville flew it at the Belmont Park meeting

ight 'Baby' of 1910. Orville, his cap reversed, stands in the centre of the group in front while Wilbur, the taller figure wearing a derby hat, holds the lower booms aft. *(Bruce Robertson* ion)

Contemporary with the D.8 was the Burgess-Dunne floatplane, one of a series of designs developed by the Burgess Company of Marblehead, Massachusetts. One such, sent to England in 1914, was unfortunately neglected and never flew again. This is a similar machine. *(Bruce Robertson Collection)*

A feature of the Everett Edgcumbe monoplane was the sharp dihedral of the wings; equally indicative of its ability was the name 'The Grasshopper', which it quickly earned. *(Author's collection)*

in the shed behind the tree on the
at work was carried out on the
mbe monoplane only six years
Wilbur and Orville's first flight. The
was used in the following year by
Paulhan during preparations for his
sful flight to Manchester which
im the 1910 *Daily Mail* prize.

or's collection)

at New York on 25 October 1910, attaining a maximum speed of some 70 mph with the aid of the only Wright V-8 engine to power an aircraft.

Today, a century after the world's first flight, aside from the replicas, there survive only six or seven genuine examples of Wright-designed aircraft. The last human contact with those long-ago days was severed in July 1977 with the passing of 92-year-old Howard French, 'the oldest commercial pilot in the world'; his pilot's licence had been signed by Orville Wright.

The world owed the Wrights an enormous debt of gratitude, but there were others who still ploughed a now lonely furrow in the search for the ideal shape of flying machine. One such was Everett Edgcumbe who perfected a Blériot-like monoplane in 1909, flying it from a field not far from the site of modern Colindale Underground Station in north London, land that would later be absorbed into Hendon Aerodrome. But his machine failed to fly successfully. Another exponent of early aviation was the vastly experienced Lieutenant J.W. Dunn, who had begun such work as a contemporary of Cody. He favoured the idea of a tailless biplane with sharply swept-back wings. Earlier there had existed the Burgess-Dunne floatplane developed by the Burgess Company of Marblehead, Massachusetts. An innovation sent to England at about the outbreak of war in 1914, it was, however, neglected and never flew again.

FIVE

PIONEERS

I believe that . . . the experiments and investigations of a large number of independent workers . . . will finally lead to accomplished flight.
                                                        Wilbur Wright, 1899

Mankind had yearned to fly from the dawn of recorded thought and probably before. Aside from such legendary figures to take to the air as Daedalus and his son Icarus, Kai Kawus of Persia in 1545BC and King Bladud (the father of King Lear, according to legend), a comparatively 'recent' pretender in 863 BC, there were those who created such practical 'flights of fancy' as Roger Bacon's in the thirteenth century, Leonardo da Vinci's designs in the fifteenth and De Lana's idea for an aerial ship two hundred years later; all early examples of mankind's long flirtation with lighter-than-air craft.

However, it was not until the mid-nineteenth century that science and engineering had developed to the point where there was a possibility of the two combining to make practicable man's attainment of controlled, powered and sustained flight, something which had hitherto been confined to the imaginings of day-dreamers and the attributes of the gods.

One of the most significant theorists of this more practical period was William Samuel Henson. In 1842 he constructed a model, based on an earlier design, for an Aerial Steam Carriage. But a model it remained, there being no attempt to construct a full-size version although Henson admired and adopted the theories of George Cayley who did cherish hopes of using his devices for human transportation. The model had been patented in the same year and was powered by a small, light steam engine. However, the machine which showed him at his most innovative is largely forgotten. This was the design for twin airscrews mounted on outriggers which he suggested, not for a conventional heavier-than-air flying machine, but for a dirigible.

Like Cayley, Henson did not confine his experiments to aviation. He studied problems associated with the new science of electricity, having trained as an engineer. A lace-maker by trade, he had been born in Nottingham, then the centre of this trade. And it was his involvement with the lace industry that had taken Henson to Somerset. There he found work at Chard where he met John Stringfellow, the pair quickly becoming friends. They shared a mutual fascination with the problems of flight and both men had made a careful study of Cayley's publications on the subject.

It was as early as 1843 when the pair decided to launch what would have been the first commercial airline in the world, the Aerial Transit Company. The more ardent of the duo foolishly made the grandiose claim that it would be possible to fly in a full-size version of the steam carriage to China from London. Indeed, it seemed a real possibility when the company, now grown to four partners, petitioned Parliament for funds to support the costs of developing a machine envisaged as a giant for its day.

Meanwhile, Henson and Stringfellow continued to experiment, chiefly with larger models propelled by a succession of light steam engines and flown from Bala Down, Chard. But these trials had to be carried out against a backdrop of growing public hostility so that Henson and Stringfellow decided to buy out

Model of a Stringfellow design for a flying machine. Its steam engine weighed only 13 lb complete with boiler and delivered 1 hp. *(Author's collection)*

their two partners. They worked on the necessary field trials of their models only under cover of darkness, despite the fact that the largest model of all, that tried in 1847, was a more refined variant of the patented design. It had a wing-span of 20 feet and was powered by a steam engine designed by Stringfellow which, although insufficiently powerful for a normal take-off without the assistance of a ramp, once airborne was to prove incapable of sustained flight. Had this test model proved viable, the full-size machine which it was planned to build would have had a span of 150 feet, a length of 84 feet 9 inches and a wing chord of 30 feet. The steam power unit was intended to be of 30-hp maximum, driving a pair of 10-foot pusher airscrews.

By now the pressures of public ridicule were increasingly troubling Henson and, having recently married, he suddenly decided to emigrate to the United States. He did not resume his aviation trials there and died at Newark, New Jersey, in 1888, leaving it to posterity to acknowledge that his was the first flying machine in history to be powered by steam.

Like his partner, John Stringfellow was a lace manufacturer. After Henson's departure, he continued with his true engineering vocation of designing light steam engines as the motive power for flying machines. The fact that his enthusiasm for aeronautics remained undiminished was proven in 1868 when he joined the (later 'Royal') Aeronautical Society founded only two years earlier. On being elected a member, Stringfellow made the announcement that successful flight by heavier-than-air machines was only a matter of years distant. His forecast was proved correct: the Wrights were to fly only thirty-five years later.

Earlier, he had made his own contributions to the first understanding of aerodynamics with the construction of a steam-driven model monoplane before seeming to lose interest. His membership of the new organisation rekindled his old interests and he contributed a model triplane to the first aeronautical exhibition which was held at Crystal Palace. Although the model could not sustain itself in the air, its configuration opened up a new line of possibilities for other designers. Interestingly, the construction of this model had first been suggested many years before by Cayley at a time (1848) when Stringfellow had still been experimenting at Chard with a 10 foot 6 inch monoplane launched along a wire and powered by steam. Its total weight was no more than an approximate 12 lb, and it was claimed that the steam pressure in the boiler could be raised to 100 lb in a time of no more than five minutes, enabling the motor to drive a pair of 21-inch propellers at 600 rpm. This 'flight' took place during June in a disused lace factory and his son has left this description of the event: 'Steam was got up and the machine started down the wire, and upon reaching the point of self detachment, it gradually rose until it reached the farther end of the room, striking a hole in the canvas placed to stop it.' John Stringfellow died in 1883 but not before repeating this flight at Cremore Gardens, Chelsea.

'La plus haute figure technique, dans le premier tiers du XIX siècle, dans celle de Sir George Cayley, le veritable inventeur de l'aéroplane.' ('The dominating technological figure of the early nineteenth century was that of Sir George Cayley, the virtual inventor of the aeroplane.') With these words the French historian Dollfus was to describe the scientific and philosophical researcher, born on 27 December 1773, who is credited with perfecting before his twentieth birthday a system of land drainage first applied on his own estates at Brompton Hall, between Pickering and Scarborough. After acceding to the title of 6th baronet and having been encouraged by his mother to have an open mind on a wide variety of subjects, his technical brilliance led him to successfully devise artificial limbs, a lightweight wheel and a 'universal railway' – a type of caterpillar tractor.

His interest in flying was first stimulated by the Montgolfier balloon when he was aged only ten, his enthusiasm later turning to a study of the properties of the air, an understanding of which he later applied to the construction of a model helicopter capable of rising to an altitude of 90 feet. This was based on a device he had seen in France in 1796, itself founded on the principles of a similar Chinese toy. It was only a comparatively short step, therefore, to the evolution of his Aerial Carriage of 1843 which had four lifting rotors that increased the pitch of their blades under centrifugal force, a further pair supplying horizontal thrust.

Six years later Sir George's interests were concentrated on the design of what today we consider to be conventional aeroplanes. He constructed a triplane with a wing area of 338 square feet and a boat-like body immediately above which was a pair of flappers for propulsion. The triplane was guided by the lower of two tail units, which was fitted with a rudder, the upper having a fixed but adjustable tailplane. It was in this machine that a test was made with a ten-year-old boy aboard, helpers running it down a slope into a light breeze in order for it to take off.

In 1853 and having perfected a larger variant of this triplane, Sir George determined to make a trial flight with his coachman, believed to have been one John Appleby, who that June was induced to take an aerial journey in the device. The inventor's granddaughter recollected the occasion:

Everyone was out on the east side [of the dale] and saw the start from close to. The coachman went in the machine and landed on the west side about

NOTICE.

Messrs. WALLIS BROS., Builders of the

"WALLBRO" (ALL BRITISH)

AEROPLANE

(THE FIRST ONE BUILT IN CAMBRIDGE)

Having had numerous requests from friends and the Public to
see their New Monoplane, they have decided to place it

ON VIEW

To the Public on

WHIT-MONDAY & TUESDAY

May 16th and 17th, 1910, from 11 to 7.30 each day, at

12, ST. BARNABAS' ROAD,

CAMBRIDGE (Three Minutes from Station).

The Machine will be Staked Down and the Motor and Tractor
SET RUNNING at 12 and 4 o'clock each day.

All who have not seen a real full-sized Flying Machine should avail
themselves of this opportunity.

Admission - - **6**d. each.

Wing Commander Kenneth H. Wallis became widely known as a specialist light helicopter display pilot, also participating in film work. In this he was following the example of his father and uncle in 1909–10 who gave exhibitions with their Wallbro Monoplane. This is an advertisement for one such exhibition. *(Author's collection via W/C Wallace)*

the same level. I think it came down a rather shorter distance than expected.

The coachman got himself clear, and when the watchers had got across he shouted, 'Please, Sir George. I wish to give notice. I was hired to drive and not to fly.' The machine was put away in the barn and I used to sit and hide in it from the governess when so inspired.

No doubt, had the outcome of this test been more auspicious, it was intended to apply the lessons learned to perfecting an aerial carriage whose design had been published the previous year, in 1852. This was to be equipped with a stabilising tail, control surfaces and a version of the lightweight wheels that had been developed earlier.

In common with other pioneers at the time, Cayley was frustrated by the lack of suitable engines. He quickly dismissed steam as being impractical, looking instead at hot-air motors first in 1799 and then, eight years later, at gunpowder motors but it proved impossible to coax these into providing sustained energy. Even so, in 1807 he was able to demonstrate a road vehicle powered by a hot-air motor in London with reasonable success.

Sir George died on 15 December 1857, aware not only that his trials had definitively proved the mistake made by other experimenters in attempting to emulate bird-flight by designing ornithopters but also that he had founded a new science, that of aerodynamics. Many of his experiments had been based on the observation of aerofoil surfaces studied at various angles when placed on a

An artist's impression of a Type 'A' in flight. *(Author's collection)*

Flight of Farman.

HENRI FARMAN.

At the 1909 Blackpool aviation meeting held at much the same time as that at Doncaster, Henry Farman, flying a machine similar to that seen in this contemporary postcard, won a prize of £2,400 flying in a gale in order not to disappoint spectators, Hubert Latham similarly taking to the air in his Antoinette monoplane. They were just two of the seven entrants who managed to leave the ground from the total of twelve present. Other British aviation meetings of late 1909 were at Brooklands, Burton and Folkestone. *(Bournemouth Library Services)*

Rolls' departure on the historic non-stop flight to Paris and back depicted over Dover Castle by aviation artist Colin Ashford. (*Courtesy C.J. Ashford GAvA FCIAD*)

'Ellehammer's Kite Aeroplane', one of the Dane's flying machines depicted by an artist of the period. (*Author's collection*)

...tiss 'D' as seen by a contemporary artist. *(Author's collection)*

...first air mail was carried in a Blériot monoplane similar to this in 1910. *(Courtesy C.J. Ashford GAvA, FCIAD)*

An Avro triplane on test over Lea Marshes as depicted by artist Colin J. Ashford GAvA, FCIAD. *(Reproduced courtesy Mrs Y. Bonham)*

Farman's Aeroplane winning the Archdeac Deutsch prize January 13th 1908.

An impression by a contemporary artist of a Farman machine winning the prize for Europe's first circular flight on 13 January 1908 in a time of 1 minute 28 seconds. The painting was based on a photograph currently in the files of the Musée de l'Air et de l'Espace. *(Author's collection)* whirling arm device which was powered by the release of a falling weight much in the manner of the launching catapult to be used by the Wright brothers less than fifty years later.

Another pioneer, but one who is undeservedly almost forgotten, was Kensington-born engineer Francis Herbert Wenham. He first became interested in the problems associated with flight on a visit to Cairo in 1858 where he observed birds. His subsequent examination of wings convinced him that it was the camber of such surfaces that contributed the greatest lift, reasoning from this that long spans presented the greatest lift. He read a paper entitled 'Aerial Locomotion' on the subject to the newly founded Aeronautical Society at its first meeting in 1866, where it was well received, many of his listeners realising that it confirmed the theories of George Cayley of some thirteen years earlier.

Casting about for a method of scientifically testing his theories, Wenham is credited with the invention in 1871 of the world's first wind tunnel, in association with John Browning. The findings of trials with its aid gave a greater understanding of his theories as to the best combination of span to aspect ratio; the final results were incorporated in a full-size glider which had five sets of superimposed wings presenting a total leading-edge length impossible to obtain with a single pair.

Wenham died aged eighty-four in 1908, having also interested himself in the newly developing worlds of steam engines, optics and photography. Yet probably his greatest contributions were those to the advancement of aviation since his findings significantly influenced the thinking of Octave Chanute and therefore those of the brothers Wright.

However, the search for controlled, heavier-than-air flight was now gathering momentum and in 1883 the former Russian naval officer Alexander Feodorovitch Mozhaiski, then aged fifty-eight, is reported to have constructed a substantial flying machine. Powered by two steam engines which produced a combined 30 hp, it had to be assisted into the air with the aid of a ramp, but reports differ as to whether aerodynamic forces or its own momentum were responsible for it becoming briefly airborne when tested near St Petersburg in 1884. It was fitted with a four-wheel undercarriage and driven by three propellers, one tractor and two pushers. Alexander was to die from natural causes six years later.

But the closing years of the nineteenth century were to be dominated among pioneer experimenters by the work of Otto Lilienthal. An engineer by training, he was the proprietor in his native Prussia of a manufacturing company producing steam engines and maritime signal equipment. Both he and his brother Gustave had shown an interest from their youth in flight, the pair having been particularly fascinated by the effortless flight of the storks that nested near their childhood home inspiring them to make childish trials with 'wings' strapped to their backs.

Even so it was to be 1891 before Otto commenced a period of experimentation with a series of gliders, eventually eighteen in number. The majority were monoplanes together with a few biplanes in which he was to make a total of over two thousand flights. The thinking behind their design was explained in Otto's book, *Bird Flight as a Basis of Aviation*, which had been published in 1889.

The planform of these gliders resembled the outline of birds, since Lilienthal believed that the eventual development of the aeroplane lay in the evolution of ornithopters – machines propelled by flapping wings. Mostly constructed from willow rods covered in waxed cotton, one contemporary writer described these gliders thus:

> So perfectly is the machine fitted together that it is impossible to find a single loose cord or brace and the cloth is everywhere under such tension that the whole machine rings like a drum when rapped with the knuckles.

He then went on to describe the sight of one of these gliders in flight – 'unforgettable . . . a man supported on huge white wings, moving high above you at racehorse speed.'

The preparation for one of these flights was anything but poetic, however. Lilienthal had first to crawl under the glider, place his arms in a pair of leather-covered, padded cuffs and seize a horizontal bar near the leading edge of the wings before running down the slope of an artificial hill which had been specially created near Berlin, and then leaping into the air, leaving his legs dangling free. In this way a flight of 750 feet had been achieved by 1893. The best flight, one of 1,000 feet, was accomplished some time later with the machine Lilienthal himself considered the most successful: the 1894 version, a monoplane with a span of 26 feet.

But gliding, however successful, was to prove lacking in any reliable means of control, the only method of doing this being for the pilot to shift the weight of his body; but a stall was almost impossible to correct and a crash practically inevitable.

It was one such mishap that was to cost Otto Lilienthal his life on the beautiful summer's day of 9 August 1896. Having risen from the Rhinower hills

A Lilienthal glider typifying the planform he favoured with a frame of willow covered in fabric. This is the 1895 version with a span of 22 feet, which differed from the variant on which Otto was killed during the following year. His brother Gustave is remembered as working on a bird-like ornithopter at Tempelhof during the summers of 1925 and 1926. *(Bruce Robertson Collection)*

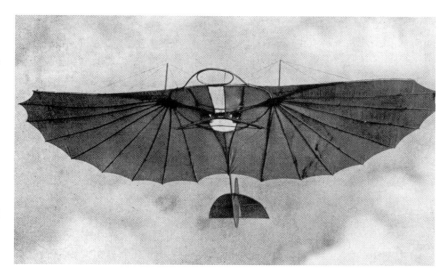

Otto Lilienthal takes a leap into the air from the slope which he used to launch himself off on a monoplane glider. *(Author's collection)*

The artificial hill near Berlin from the slope of which Lilienthal would run to gain assistance into the air. In this instance he is doing so in a biplane version of his glider design. *(Author's collection)*

near Stollen, a spot he had used for the past five years, then over the prominences of Gollenberg, at an altitude of only 50 feet the monoplane glider he was flying dropped its starboard wing after a stall, lost lift and side-slipped before crashing into the ground, breaking Otto's back. He died the following day. A copy of the reports he left is said to have reached the Wrights and been studied before the construction of their first glider, but unfortunately the data proved faulty and of little assistance to the Americans. Ironically, despite the superb skill he displayed in flying his gliders, Lilienthal realised that the crude method of controlling them was inadequate, and he is recorded as having designed a controllable rear elevator for his devices; unfortunately, this had yet to be fitted to any of his machines by the time of his death, when he was working instead on the development of a carbonic gas aero-engine.

Another experimenter employing a glider two years before the bold Prussian's death was the wealthy, Georgia-born Augustus Moore Herring. He left New York, where his parents had moved, in order to receive his secondary education in Europe. Here he became fluent in French and German before returning home and beginning studies at the Stevens Institute of Technology some time in the 1880s, having an ambition to become an engineer. It was at about the same time that he reportedly had his treatise on flying rejected, despite having based it in part on the two gliders he had built. However, neither of these was successful, so he purchased a Lilienthal glider in 1894, having several copies made.

During the same year Herring was to meet Octave Chanute from whom he accepted an offer of employment. As his assistant, Herring accompanied Chanute on trials with flying machines on the Indiana Dunes east of Chicago, and although he showed some promise as a glider pilot, the two parted when the older man became irritated by his helper.

Herring now obtained backing for his experiments from a prosperous New York source and began work on a powered version of his earlier glider design. Although this had been satisfactory in its original form so that the promise of a version fitted with a motor seemed bright, mastery of the practical aspects proved less hopeful. Wishing for the benefit of his expertise, Herring reopened his professional contacts with Chanute who took him to visit the Wright brothers at Kitty Hawk and they were approached with the offer of a partnership. However, an awareness, matched by Herring, that success was not far off, coupled with both Wilbur and Orville's immediate distrust of him, meant the suggestion was politely declined.

The fortune inherited from Herring senior was now in danger of being entirely dissipated due to the son's profligate business methods. Desperate for a new financial backer and despite the obvious lack of promise of his series of experiments, Herring finally approached Glen Curtiss, arch-rival of the Wrights, claiming to hold a number of patents applicable to flying. Alas, he held no such patents and Curtiss, not before signing the entire factory over to Herring, eventually realised that he had been duped and managed to break up the organisation.

Herring died in 1927, his place in the history of flight due solely to his association with the genuine pioneers of the period. Although his tender to supply a military aeroplane for the US Army was accepted on 10 February 1908, the promised machine failed to materialise.

Hiram Stevens Maxim, an American born on 5 February 1840 at Sangerville, Maine, settled at West Norwood, south London, in 1881, took British citizenship in 1900 and received a knighthood from Queen Victoria in the following year. A professional inventor, he made a fortune from his Maxim machine-gun two years later, before becoming interested in powered flight. This was, no doubt, due in part to his father's attempts to perfect a two-rotor

Sir Hiram Maxim's gigantic flying machine of 1894. *(Author's collection)*

helicopter before finally deciding in favour of fixed wings, Hiram following suit with a helicopter design of his own in 1872.

Deciding to follow the path trodden by his father, Hiram first designed two light but powerful steam engines capable of delivering some 180 hp, sufficient to power the monster biplane when it was tested in the grounds of Baldwyns Park at Bexley, Kent. Here he lodged at the mansion and had a massive hangar erected for his 3-ton aeroplane which was first tested by running along a fixed track from which, in July 1894, it certainly lifted itself, despite a crew of three, within the limits imposed by the guide rails, travelling a distance of some 600 feet on its best run.

Construction of this machine had begun three years earlier and had proved expensive, Hiram augmenting the costs by meeting his financial backers with a personal contribution of £20,000. The ensuing machine was certainly impressive, having a span of 125 feet and a length of 104 feet with twin directly driven 17-foot propellers, the gigantic hexagonal centre section alone being capable of carrying a variety of outer wing panels and measuring 40 feet across. Unfortunately, this mammoth flying machine showed no promise of sustained flight, despite Hiram's aside that 'If the domestic goose can fly, so can man'.

The success, however limited, of his Bexley trials was in part due to his earlier study of the new and little understood science of aerodynamics with the aid of the swinging arm favoured by so many pioneers. Although for a time Hiram had tended to refer to his massive contraption as the 'First Kite of War', he was heard later to admit uncharacteristically, 'I rather overdid it at Baldwyns Park'. Yet he clearly had sufficient faith in his ideas to resume similar trials with a new biplane at Crayford, Kent, in 1910. These fared no better than the first and were likewise abandoned. However, Maxim took these disappointing results in his stride as he had the first set and turned to other work. He died on 24 November 1916, having retired five years earlier with 150 patents to his credit. The funeral, held at 11.30 a.m. four days later, was attended by numerous mourners, their large number testifying to the esteem in which he was held by so many. Included among his friends were the distinguished authors Rudyard Kipling and H.G. Wells, the latter having consulted him before embarking on *The Argonauts of the Air*, published in 1895.

Among Maxim's contemporaries was the French-American Dr Octave Chanute. Born in Paris on 18 February 1832, Octave was purely an active experimenter since he was a railroad engineer by profession. He had the good fortune to become a friend of the Wright brothers, who had been attracted by his book, *Progress in Flying Machines*, which was the first comprehensive history of heavier-than-air flight. From 1896 onwards he devoted much of his spare time to the design of Lilienthal-type gliders some of which were multi-winged or had pivoting mainplanes. When the gliders were test-flown on the shores of Lake Michigan, Augustus M. Herring and William Avery acted as pilots on several occasions.

Before his death in 1910 an unfortunate rift between Chanute and the Wrights took place as a consequence of the misguided belief that his influence over the brothers had been greater than in fact it was; the matter was eventually resolved, seen for the misinterpretation that it was.

It was at about this time, too, that there were the first indications that France would shortly emerge as the European centre of aeronautics. An experimenter with a newly acquired interest in flying was the prosperous, 32-year-old engineer Clement Ader, at the time working on telephones. It would be a further nine years before he constructed his first aeroplane, the 'Eole'. This resembled nothing more than a giant wheeled bat, even to its folding wings, spanning 46 feet and weighing 652 lb. With this, on 9 October 1890 at Armainvilliers he achieved a significant 'hop' – 9 feet above the ground for a distance of 165 feet with the aid of a four-cylinder, 20-hp light steam engine driving a four-blade tractor airscrew.

Great secrecy surrounded this event so that it was a long time before the crash that concluded it became public knowledge. But even then work was proceeding on a larger, similar replacement, the 'Avion II'. This had two airscrews, each driven by a separate copy of the original engine, now giving 29 hp each. A development of this machine, the 52-foot 'Avion III', was demonstrated to the military authorities at Satory on 12 and 14 October 1897 as the direct result of a personal invitation from M. de Freycinet, Minister for War. This was the culmination of a contract, signed on 3 February 1892, for a

Clement Ader's 'Avion' showing its bat-like lines and twin airscrews. *(The British Library)*

two-seat machine capable of carrying 165 lb of explosives (although the machine had to be flown as a single seater to allow this), with an operational altitude of several hundred feet and the capacity for a minimum duration of six hours. However, although flights of slightly more than 328 yards distance were rumoured – on doubtful authority – to have taken place, a broadside gust of wind brought all to an end. His personal fortune now severely depleted and an application for support from the military authorities having been refused, Ader destroyed all his drawings and the remains of 'Eole', preserved only one of the 'Avion' machines and withdrew from the field.

Ader died on 3 May 1925, having earlier published *L'Aviation militaire*, a work in which he accurately foretold many of the subsequent advances in aeronautics, with the result that for a time Ader was frequently described as the 'father of aviation'. He lived to see the dispatch of a mission to the United States by the Minister of War in 1906 with the aim of obtaining a manufacturing licence for the Wright biplane. Within two years, terms were agreed, the resultant work being entrusted to the Compagnie General de Navigation Aérienne. General Roques, the first French Inspecteur-General de l'Aéronautique Militaire, delegated to Commandant Bouttieaux the task of supervising tests of the new machines.

At much the same time as the contract had been signed, however, the French authorities declared the Wright motors inadequate, so that the original output of 12 hp was raised to 30 hp as the result of modifications introduced by Bariquand et Marre; but how many of these new power units were initially fitted is not known. In addition, many of the French Wrights, the first of which were handed over on 10 June 1910, had been scheduled to have rear moving tailplanes and wheeled undercarriages. However, the latter was absent from the first aeroplane delivered to the French Army, a Curtiss-Wright which was immediately tested by Capitaine Eteve. Its additional stabiliser was of the automatic variety, personally designed and developed by the same capitaine. Two Wrights, in addition to a pair of Farmans and a Blériot XI, had been ordered in September 1909, a Wright-Bariquand being ordered soon afterwards.

Born at Lyons on 8 February 1862, Ferdinand Ferber entered the Ecole Polytechnique twenty years later. On joining the Army, he rose from the ranks to become a lieutenant, eventually becoming a capitaine commanding a battery of the Alpine artillery at Nice between 1901 and 1904. He was elevated to the rank of a Chevalier of the Légion d'Honneur in 1905.

Meanwhile, in 1899, he had begun to take an interest in aviation pursuing the line of Lilienthal's trials, forming a friendship with Chanute and

...powered flight was achieved a certain commonality of layout was evident by 1910, as typified by this Grahame White 'Baby'. Opinions varied as to the viability of monoplanes over ...s. *(Bruce Robertson Collection)*

constructing a moderately successful glider, at first with monoplane wings and later, in 1902, as a biplane. Widening his research, two years later he constructed a new glider at Chalais-Meudon; this was fitted with a 12-hp motor, only to have his hopes of developing it dashed when the War Office refused financial support.

Returning to civilian life, Ferber nevertheless continued his aerial investigations with further gliders, the ninth of which was a monoplane powered by a 50-hp motor, and it was in this that he was to make his first successful flights at some time after 1903. These flights were followed by others in a Voisin type, this being the machine with which he won several awards during May 1909, awards offered by the Aero Club of France for a 547-foot flight. In June he won the Roland-Gosselin prize and the Archdeacon Cup, among others, in July successfully competing at Rheims. But sadly 'de Rue' was destined to die not long afterwards, in a fatal crash at Boulogne on 19 September 1909 when the aircraft which he was testing turned over on soft ground and crushed him.

Capitaine Ferber made few material contributions to the advancement of controlled, sustained heavier-than-air flight. However, he was involved with the design of the Antoinette series of aeroplanes and kept to his resolve never to give up any line of investigation on which he had embarked until satisfied or proven unavailing.

Arguably, these qualities of courage and perseverance amply describe the British pioneer Percy Sinclair Pilcher. 'A most lovable character' according to

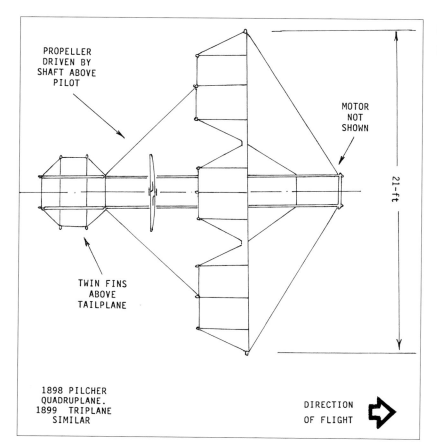

PROPELLER
DRIVEN BY
SHAFT ABOVE
PILOT

MOTOR
NOT
SHOWN

21-ft

TWIN FINS
ABOVE
TAILPLANE

1898 PILCHER
QUADRUPLANE.
1899 TRIPLANE
SIMILAR

DIRECTION
OF FLIGHT

Pilcher's quadruplane of 1898.

(*Author*)

Chanute, although generally remembered primarily as a gliding experimenter, like the Wrights Pilcher saw this as little more than a means of addressing the problems associated with mastering powered flight. To that end he had set about designing a suitable motor shortly before his death, having, again like the Wright brothers, been frustrated in the search for a commercially available power unit. This Pilcher motor, which may have been fitted but not used on his final glider, was a light, 4-hp oil (petrol) motor, a unique idea at the time.

Born in the City of Bath in January 1866 and only thirteen years old when he joined the Royal Navy in 1879, Pilcher left the service in 1885 as a lieutenant, to concentrate on an engineering career. Having proved himself hard-working and with an understanding of aviation and maritime matters, in 1893 he was appointed Assistant Lecturer in Naval Architecture and Marine Engineering at Glasgow University. Three years later, he became a consultant to Maxim during preparations for the construction of the second of Sir Hiram's aircraft.

Early in 1895 Pilcher had also embarked on aircraft construction, beginning to build a monoplane glider with an enormous dihedral angle. The machine came to be known as 'The Bat', a hang-glider with an area of 150 square feet, weighing 45 lb without its pilot. But before this was complete he visited Otto Lilienthal in Berlin in April 1895, making a number of glides under Otto's direction. Returning home, he attempted flight with his own glider at Cardross on the banks of the Clyde in June of the same year, later adding a tailplane as Lilienthal had suggested.

Encouraged by the success of this first project, 'The Beetle', another monoplane with a ten-sided planform to the wings was built and flown, also in 1895. This version had an area increased by 20 square feet and weighing tare 35 lb more than 'The Bat', the new machine going to the opposite extreme from its predecessor in having no dihedral.

By September, however, Pilcher had returned to experimenting with his first glider and on the 12th 'The Bat', its excessive dihedral now reduced, proved itself capable of hovering – presumably with the aid of a thermal – at an altitude of 12 feet for 3 seconds. His third glider, 'The Gull', quickly followed late in 1896, and although weighing only 55 lb tare, it was considerably larger with a wing area of 300 square feet. Although clearly inspired by the Lilienthal designs, it was described as having 'too much lift', being flyable only under

Pilcher's final glider was 'The Hawk', seen here and still preserved in the Royal Scottish Museum. *(The British Library)*

calm conditions. This claim taxed Pilcher to the point where he attempted to fly it irrespective of the weather, but after two crashes he abandoned it, not even bothering to repair the final damage.

All these models would today be described as hang-gliders, and Pilcher's last design was known as 'The Hawk'. Its appearance strongly resembled that of the German machines on which it was based and it introduced the innovation of a slim, folding boom to support the tailplane for storage convenience, and a wheeled undercarriage. The span of this latest aircraft was 23 feet 4 inches giving an area of 180 square feet with a weight of 50 lb; its best performance was attained on 20 June 1897 with a record glide 750 feet in length.

Launched on each occasion with the aid of a tow-line, this glider was flown many times during 1896/7 at Eynsford, Kent, mostly achieving distances in the region of 200 yards. A particularly important demonstration was planned to take place on 30 September 1899 for Henniker Heaton MP at Stanford Hall near Rugby, the home of Lord Braye.

On that occasion, the tow-off was by means of a pair of horses, the first two attempts to become airborne failing when at each try the tow parted as the

Pilcher, assisted by his loyal sister Ella, poses with his second glider 'The Beetle' at Cardross in 1895. This was his second and slightly larger than the first 'Bat' design with a wing area of 170 square feet. It was also some 25 lb heavier and was fitted with a tail unit from the beginning. (*Author's collection*)

uthful Dutchman Anthony Fokker at the
s of a variant of the first 'Spinne'
r) which he designed and flew. The
of aviation in the opening years of the
2th century was typified by such
s. (Author's collection via W/C Wallace)

strain was taken up. At the third attempt 'The Hawk' had risen no more than 30 feet when the bamboo tail support suddenly snapped, the result, it was later claimed, of the glider having been left out overnight in the rain so that the wooden members became saturated. Pilcher was severely injured in the fall, dying two days later on 2 October; he was just thirty-three.

Stored and subsequently repaired by T.W.A. Clarke, glider-builders of 14 Union Street, Kingston-on-Thames, Surrey, 'The Hawk' was exhibited at the 1909 Travel Exhibition at Olympia, London and is currently displayed in the Royal Scottish Museum, Edinburgh. Here it still serves to impress by reason of its wheeled undercarriage, a dihedral which raises the wing-tips some 4 feet and its controllable tail unit. Small wonder that it was once credited with a glide for a distance of 250 feet across a Kent valley.

Had he lived, some claim that Pilcher may well have succeeded in making a controlled, powered and sustained flight before the Wrights. This belief was in the light of the fact that during the previous year Pilcher had confirmed his intentions to construct a powered machine for a pusher design with a propeller of some 4 feet in diameter driven from an engine situated in front by means of a lengthy shaft. Plans to build the quadruplane which had originally been considered having now been abandoned, the envisaged powered machine, known as 'The Duck' was, he wrote in the following year, to be 'very similar to "The Hawk" . . . [with an estimated flying speed of] about 30 miles per hour'.

SIX

TRIALS

You must mount a machine [like an unknown horse] and become acquainted with its tricks by actual trial.

Wilbur Wright, 1901

Either by coincidence or from a desire to emulate the Wright brothers' achievement, the first years of the twentieth century were particularly rich in practical experimenters in the art of controlled flight, their brief biographies being told here in the chronological order of the pinnacle of their success in their particular specialist field.

One such, Gustav Whitehead, born Gustav Weisskopf and a Bavarian immigrant to the United States, went one better than the claim to have enjoyed success at the same time as the two on Kill Devil Hills; rather it is alleged that he achieved flight before them, in 1901, when he commenced building his 'No. 21'. Tested before dawn in August that year, it gained an altitude of 50 feet before completing a trip of one and a half miles over the Connecticut countryside, the subsequent 'No. 22' bettering this range by half a mile at an altitude of 200 feet. In 1934, seven years after the death of Whitehead, a witness claimed to have been a passenger in a similar steam-powered aircraft in 1899, this flight ending when the machine collided with a three-storey building, he added.

The whole question of the Whitehead flights was the subject of serious investigation by Professor J.B. Crane in 1935 and included interviews with witnesses of the trials, some of which had taken place in the streets of Bridgeport. But little consistency was found, altitudes being stated as anything between 4 and 25 feet, while quoted distances travelled varied between 60 and 300 feet. Among those interviewed, Dr Crane was lucky to meet John Fekete who had assisted Whitehead to construct his power-plants. Fekete is described as of 'above average education and intelligence' so it is noteworthy that his recollections were of little more than hops to a height of about 20 feet from which the several contraptions glided to the ground.

The 'Double Monoplane' of Commander Sir Walter Windham RN at Wembley Park. The commander was also responsible for organising, in India, the world's first air-mail service. *(Author's collection)*

Dr Samuel P. Langley, Secretary of the Smithsonian Institution from 1887 to 1906, interested himself in the question of flight despite being ridiculed by many. This seemed justified when in October 1903 his 'Aerodrome' flying machine crashed into the Potomac while being launched from his houseboat. *(Author's collection)*

Today, the efforts of Gustav Whitehead tend to be regarded as no more than 'flights of fancy', but one mystery remains. What precisely was shown in an indistinct photograph described as being of 'a large birdlike machine propelled by compressed air!' and published in 1906, a device for which even Gustav himself made no claims!

The claims to aeronautical achievement of Samuel Pierpont Langley, however, enjoy firmer foundations. An early head of the Smithsonian Institution, he first became interested in heavier-than-air flight towards the end of the nineteenth century, flying his first giant model machine in 1896. During the following seven years he built a further six; of these, one proved capable of an altitude of 3,000 feet and so excited the interest of the US War Department that Langley was invited to construct a full-size machine, assisted by a grant of $50,000.

Curiously to modern ears, this tandem-wing monoplane was termed as an 'Aerodrome', a description chosen because Langley thought that the word 'plane' gave an impression of an uncurved surface. Attempts to launch this machine were made from the top of a houseboat on the Potomac River with the assistance of Charles Manley who, although later the pilot designate, was at first employed to oversee the work of Stephen Balzer, the engine designer. Manley later redesigned the 8-hp rotary power unit to become a 42-hp radial engine, although it was claimed that the weight was a mere 208 lb.

The Langley Hydroplane on the shores of the Potomac. *(Bruce Robertson Collection)*

There were several variants of this design, the best known being described simply as 'No. 5'; it was steel-framed and weighed 830 lb with a pilot aboard. The first trial launch of such a machine was scheduled for 7 October 1903, but unfortunately the aircraft struck a protrusion on the launching vessel and plunged into the water, nearly drowning Manley. Subsequent repairs prevented a further attempt until 8 December, with similar disastrous results. To this was added the embarrassment of the 'Aerodrome' being torn in half as the result of over-enthusiastic attempts by a tug crew to salvage it after darkness had fallen. Nine days later the Wrights made their first flight.

The following year saw the appearance on the aviation scene in New Zealand of Richard William Pearse, a farmer with some engineering knowledge who enjoyed the nickname of 'Bamboo Dick'. He made an unassisted attempt to fly in March 1903 or 1904. (This after he had moved to Milton in Upper Waitohi, Central South Island, where his best-documented attempts to fly were made.) He first took the flying machine to the top of a slope in order to gain momentum for a take-off; results were mixed, sometimes taking the form of no more than a hop, at others culminating in complete failure and a crash (the first such endeavour is said to have ended in a gorse hedge!). Power was by means of petrol motors, although the identity of these is in some doubt, Pearse seemingly having attempted to design such units himself.

Richard Pearse photographed in 1903 aged twenty-five. *(AHSNZ)*

Known to his neighbours as something of a recluse, Pearse was later to become a legend, the belief that he had successfully flown gaining credibility with the passage of time. Faith in his achievement appeared to be endorsed by the fact that Pearse registered a patent as early as 1906, which led some to suggest that the New

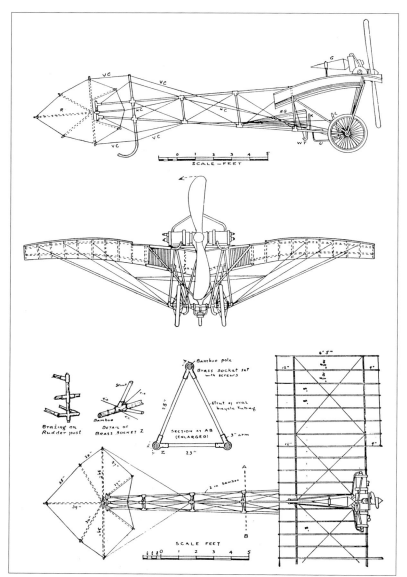

'La Demoiselle'. A contemporary general arrangement drawing publi[shed]
shortly after the appearance of the type in 1909.
Key to side view:
MP.   Main plane with radiator which was lying underneath
HC.   Wires to actuate rudder   VC.   Elevator control wires
L.   Elevator control   G.   Fuel tank   R.   Rudder
K.   Wing-warping lever in pocket in back of pilot's coat
U.   Pilot's seat   WT. Tube for wing-warping wires
(Author's collection)

Zealander had achieved flight before the Wrights. This claim was made by some
for a number of years until, in 1915, Pearse himself stated that the attempted
flights of 1904 had all resulted in failure; although an interesting revelation was
that the machine incorporated such novel features as ailerons and a tricycle
landing gear with a steerable nose-wheel. Ten years later, now aged forty-eight
and having seen military service during the First World War, Pearse was again at
work, this time on a STOL machine incorporating a tilting engine and a variable-

pitch airscrew. He died in 1953 leaving a number of interesting technical artefacts, the majority of which have been salvaged and preserved.

Another, better-remembered experimenter was the Brazilian Alberto Santos-Dumont. The son of a wealthy coffee planter, the young man lived in France where, in 1897 at the age of twenty-four, he first became interested in balloon flight. His balloons were soon fitted with small petrol engines, but it was not until 1901 and the appearance of his sixth design, which won him the Deutsch de la Meurthe prize for making a round trip from Saint Cloud to the Eiffel Tower, that he became something of a national hero.

His entry into the field of the heavier-than-air machine was not an immediate success since he used a large under-powered canard built for him by the Voisin brothers. It refused to fly satisfactorily when tested on 14 September 1906, achieving a flight time of only 8 seconds. Only when it was fitted with an Antoinette motor of a little over double the horsepower of the first was success achieved, on 12 November, making it the first successful flight in Europe.

A mercurial little man subject to swift changes of mood, Santos-Dumont enjoyed the popularity this gave him, but when Wilbur Wright visited France in 1908 he is said to have felt personally eclipsed with the result that he began the design of a miniature aircraft, 'La Demoiselle'. This proving a success in 1909, he donated it to the public. Alas, this was to be his final gesture to the advancement of aviation, for the following year he was diagnosed with multiple sclerosis and went home to Brazil. Here, the news

The light aircraft designed by Santos-Dumont. It was known as 'La Demoiselle' and was his nineteenth. *(Author's collection)*

The Santos-Dumont 14bis Canard design. (*Author's collection*)

that the flying machine which he loved was being employed as a weapon of destruction in the First World War increasingly depressed him and this together with the growing horrors of his malady drove him to hang himself in 1932.

Tragedies notwithstanding, this period was rich in the endeavours of amateur experimenters who made their contributions to the science of flight. Of these, one of the less well known was Baden Fletcher Smyth Baden-Powell, brother of the founder of the Boy Scouts. A major in the Army, he became interested in powered flight in 1909, exhibiting in that year the 'Scout' or 'Midge' successor to his 22-foot-span 'Quadruplane' and powered by a 50-hp Antoinette motor. The machine, displayed at Olympia, reappeared later still fitted with a three-cylinder, 12-hp Buchet engine. Major Baden-Powell, already a veteran of man-lifting kites* and balloons, had flown with Wilbur Wright in 1908, only the second Englishman to do so.

---

* Man-lifting kites were much older than this in the West, Martha Pocock of Bristol having ascended to 300 feet in one of her father's kites in about 1827. She would later become the wife of Dr W.G. Grace, the cricketer.

...illon and Clouzy biplane about to be tested on Epsom Downs, Surrey, on 11 April 1907 by co-designer M. Guillon. Designed for a prone pilot and powered by a 20-hp four-cylinder driving a 5-foot diameter airscrew, the machine had single-surface wings. Although proving incapable of flight, it did reach a speed of 20 mph on the ground. *(Courtesy Taylor)*

Like Santos-Dumont, Jacob Christian Hansen Ellehammer was to win acclaim in aviation outside his own country. A Dane by birth, some of his early work was carried out in Germany, the year 1904 seeing his introduction to the world of aviation by the production of an air-cooled three-cylinder radial motor generating 9 hp. Although this never powered an aeroplane in flight it was fitted to Ellehammer's first aeroplane which was built at Copenhagen in 1905. This was a monoplane with triangular wings attached to a large centre section in the form of a semi-circular tunnel, the motor powering a propeller made from canvas stretched over a frame via a belt drive. This machine was tested on the island of Lindholm in 1905, a location so small that a trial take-off in a straight line was impossible and the aircraft had to be tethered to fly from a circular track of 33 feet diameter and 1,969 feet circumference.

As in the rest of Europe, aviation was to advance swiftly in Germany, signalled by the development of such types as the Grade monoplane, designed by Hans Grade. This was the first to be produced and was a tractor triplane introduced in 1908. Its clumsy appearance gave way to a wonderfully simple monoplane in the following year. *(Author's collection)*

Another example of German design, one of the bird-like Taube (Dove) types produced by the Etrich organisation, Alfred Friedrich bringing his example marked 'D2' to Hendon in 1913. The type was extremely stable although at the cost of speed. *(Bruce Robertson Collection)*

The Ellehammer machine of 1905. (Author's collection)

Longitudinal control only was maintained, this being achieved by the weight of the engine and pilot which acted as a pendulum swinging beneath the wings and activating the rear elevator, the movement of this weight combination being adjustable in flight. The first flight of aircraft No. 2, a semi-biplane variant of the first, was made during the summer of 1906, a modified version of this machine later travelling a distance of about 138 feet at a height of some 20 inches on 12 September of the same year. Since the machine was still tethered and had a fixed rudder, this trial is not regarded as a genuine flight; true flight is not considered to have been achieved until 1907, when Ellehammer's No. 3 – the first man-carrying triplane in the world – powered by his excellent 30-hp radial motor, made a number of significant hops. The No. 3 seems to have been the most successful of this designer's machines and although several others are known, being described as Nos 5, 6 and 7, they were relative failures and little or nothing is recorded about them.

Meanwhile in France a fresh name was emerging in aviation, that of the Voisin brothers, Gabriel and Charles, the younger by eight years. Gabriel Voisin is known to have been acquainted with both Ader and Ferber, who suggested that he made his interest in flight known to Ernest Archdeacon. Thus it was that on 29 May 1908 Archdeacon achieved the distinction of becoming Europe's first air passenger. He was then himself currently experimenting with construction of a Wright-type glider with the result that Gabriel was employed as a pilot. Gabriel and Archdeacon soon formed a syndicate for the

Actor Robert Loraine about to attempt the first crossing of the Irish Sea from Holyhead on 11 September 1910, only to be forced down some 60 yards from his goal. With the outbreak of war he was to become a major in the Royal Flying Corps. As early as 1910, aircraft were being thought of in terms of sport. *(Bruce Robertson Collection)*

manufacture of gliders, two new ones being completed before the end of 1905. Since the second was made to fulfil an order from Blériot, it led to the formation of a new partnership to produce aircraft, although by now Voisin was working for Santos-Dumont who had his type 14 *bis* under construction. However, the partnership with Blériot was not to last, Gabriel quickly forming a new one, Aeroplanes Voisin Frères, in collaboration with Charles. Their second machine, ordered by Delagrange, who later became the chief designer to the Nieuport organisation, flew in March 1907 in what was the initial success for the first firm founded for the construction of heavier-than-air machines.

Between 1907 and 1913, a succession of machines was produced, including a number of an experimental nature, probably the most famous being the Voisin Types LA and LA.S, pusher. Based on a design by the brothers first shown before the First World War, they were steel-framed and employed during that conflict for training, reconnaissance and as a two-seat night bomber.

Samuel Franklin Cody's bluff, genial, hard-working, brave and kindly nature brought him immense popularity and respect. Born S.F. Cowdery at Birdville, Texas, on 6 March 1816, he later developed into a 6 foot 3 inch, 15 stone giant. As a young man, he was a fine shot with both rifle and revolver, sitting a fast horse with easy confidence. It was this latter talent that brought him to England, in charge of a consignment of fifty horses to be delivered to the Sloane Square address of dealer John Blackburn Davis, whose customers included King Edward VII, great-grandfather of Queen Elizabeth II.

Settling in Great Britain, in 1899 he toured Europe with his Wild West show before beginning flight trials at the Royal Aircraft Establishment, Farnborough. His first flights were with early airships from which he progressed to aeroplanes; he told a press reporter in the year the Wrights first flew successfully, 'I hope at no very distant date to play an important part in the complete conquest of the air.'

Those early aeroplanes had evolved out of the kites built for military use at Farnborough. A visit to the production sheds is recalled by a visitor of the time, who was shown 'the hall, some 200 feet long and 60 feet wide, [which] was a hive of industry with an indefinable smell, composed of glue and canvas, and hemp and dust . . .

S.F. Cody in European attire. *(Real Photographs)*

[while] the incessant chatter of sewing machines presented a constant background to the bustle of human activity.'

Cody's first flying machine took the form of a biplane glider. Little more than one of his observation kites with a wheeled undercarriage and stabilising surfaces fore and aft, it was test-flown in 1907, without a pilot, with a 15-hp Buchet motor, on several occasions achieving a duration of almost 5 minutes over Farnborough Common. This was followed in the same year by a more

Cody's Michelin Cup biplane in flight showing its separate ailerons, substantial landing skid and ancillary wheels on the lower wing-tips. *(Bruce Robertson Collection)*

ambitious aircraft with a superficial resemblance to Wright layout and known as the British Army Aeroplane No. 1 (not to be confused with Cody's Military Trials Biplane). Unusually in an age of almost universal wing-warping, it had Esnault-Pelterie-type ailerons, and although these showed promise, they were discarded soon after tests began on 19 September 1908, a short hop being achieved ten days later.

These tests were carried out in an atmosphere of great secrecy, albeit difficult to maintain since the machine was hardly inconspicuous, having a wingspan of 52 feet. Although essentially a design intended for development and with frequent alterations resulting, it was used to set up a record for distance and duration in a straight line at an altitude of 30 feet on 14 May 1909. It covered 1½ miles at 25 mph on 18 June and made a circular flight of 4 miles on 21 July. Although the hoped-for crowning achievement with this biplane would have been to win the £1,000 *Daily Mail* prize in October, an accident prevented Cody entering the contest. (Unfortunately, it was especially to qualify for participation in this event that Sam had earlier taken British citizenship.)

Cody was eventually to be responsible for a total of seven aircraft designs, the Army Aeroplane No. 1 being followed in 1910 by a biplane intended for entry into the Michelin Cup. Although in the end it was not entered for this

£4,000 prize, which involved a flight into Europe from Britain, participation in a subsidiary £500 contest resulted in a successful 94½ mile flight round Laffan's Plain accomplished in 2 hours and 24 minutes.

Cody's successful design was his Circuit of Britain Biplane, which owed much to the earlier 1910 aircraft but with the addition of twin rudders and 60-hp Green engine. It won several prizes, but the most significant event with which it was connected is now little remembered. This took place on 27 January 1912 when four passengers added their weight to that of the pilot to make a total load of 738 lb over a distance of 7 miles at Laffan's Plain. An altitude of 100 feet was achieved with the aid of a 120-hp Austro-Daimler motor. This motor was of the same type to power the next Cody design, a monoplane intended for entry into the Military Aircraft trials of that year, but it was unfortunately never completed and was wrecked in July after collision with a cow.

Now aged fifty-one, so that his colleagues affectionately referred to him as 'Papa Cody', he won the British Military Aeroplane Trials in 1912 and was still

The Anderson monoplane built by the Farnborough Aviation Works, Kent, in 1910 and clearly resembling the Blériot monoplane. *(Courtesy W. Morton)*

almost completely financially self-supporting. He then went on to design a massive floatplane which he was in the process of testing with a wheeled undercarriage on 7 August the following year when he was persuaded to take aloft a number of passengers at a cost of £5 per head.

One of these companions was the former Hampshire cricketer, W.H.B. Evans. The aircraft had reached some 3,000 feet above Cove Common when the wings suddenly buckled flinging out the two men, who died instantly as a result of the fall. Such was their grief at the loss of a great man that, four days later, the Army gave him a full military funeral with every regiment in the British Army represented in the cortège. More than fifty thousand civilians attended to say adieu to 'Colonel' Sam Cody. His adopted son Frank survived him, to die in action in the conflict that was to engulf the world only a year later.

Mention should be made of a much less known experimenter who was a contemporary of Cody. John Anderson was a nurseryman who had settled at Farnborough, Kent, around 1908 after moving south from Cumberland. Here, in the fields beside the Hastings road, he built and experimented with a Blériot-like monoplane during 1910.

Tailplane, port wing, rudder, fuselage and undercarriage leg of the Anderson machine in store at the Farnborough Aviation Works. The poster on the far wall reads 'Wings constructed with scientific accuracy'. *(Courtesy W. Morton)*

Although interest in aviation was now increasing in Europe and the United States in the years following the Wrights' success, there were still many financiers who were in a position to widen that popularity but hesitated to do so due to distrust of the new means of travel, some because of scepticism, others in the belief that the new sport was nothing more than a passing fad confined to the wealthy, and one which would soon fade away.

There were, however, a few who took a more enlightened view. One of these was Ernest Archdeacon, Chairman of the Aero Club of France soon after the dawn of the twentieth century. A man made wealthy by his law practice, when the aviation craze swept Europe he did not hesitate to encourage its growth, sponsoring aviation meetings and competitions. His greatest achievement in this field was probably the promotion of the events connected with the sensational Rheims Week of 1909, the first such gathering in history and one that brought together the very men whose interest, effort and technological skill would shape the future of humanity.

It is claimed that for Archdeacon, it was simply the fact that he became the first air passenger in Europe on 29 May 1908 that changed his attitude to flying. Even if it is true that the experience clinched his point of view, Ernest had already enjoyed connections with the new art of navigating the skies when he gave financial support to Gabriel Voisin for his early glider trials. This generosity was again evident on the establishment of the Syndicat d'Aviation, later to provide the foundations on which Voisin Frerès was built. Archdeacon's enthusiasm for aviation also prompted him to help finance the experiments of Capitaine Ferdinand Ferber, who in turn played no small part in making France the centre of European aviation prior to 1914.

Meanwhile American aviation was not being shaped alone by the Wright brothers, instrumental though their founding work had been. The new entrant into the field – some even claiming that he was Wilbur and Orville's 'arch-rival' – was Glenn Hammond Curtiss. Born at Hammondsport, New York (a place that took its name from one of his ancestors), he showed a natural ability for things mechanical, no doubt triggered by the bicycle craze that swept the world, the same mania that had decided the Wrights to set up their own bicycle repair and production business. Like the Wright brothers, Curtiss had entered trade through a very different door, in his case as an employee at Eastman's Kodak factory. In common with his later rivals, Curtiss eventually began with bicycle manufacture, later widening its scope to include motorcycles. Soon, Glenn was racing his machines, winning the World Land Speed Record in 1907 at 136 mph on a machine powered by an engine of his own design.

Contemporary photograph of the Curtiss 'D'. The disputed inter-gap ailerons may just be made out. *(Bruce Robertson Collection)*

The Curtiss 'June Bug', which won the trophy for the 'First Public Flight in the USA' presented by *Scientific American* magazine on 4 July 1908. *(Bruce Robertson Collection)*

r Curtiss 'Silver Dart', its appearance differing from that of the 'June Bug' mainly due to its having a biplane forward elevator. *(Bruce Robertson Collection)*

It was this success that brought him to the attention of Alexander Graham Bell, who was about to found the Aerial Experiment Association (ALA). Curtiss became responsible for the power unit for the 'June Bug' aircraft of 1908 and, the following year, set up America's first aircraft manufacturing company. In 1911, he was responsible for the first practical hydroplane, the first in a series of such aircraft for which the firm was known throughout the First World War. Lengthy litigation, chiefly with Herring who was also involved with the organisation, hastened his death in 1930, at the comparatively early age of fifty-two.

A name which quickly became known in the aviation world in the first decade of the twentieth century was that of Léon Morane. When less than twenty-five years of age, he had already been Louis Blériot's competition manager, a post he held until 1911. Together with his brother, younger by only a year, and Gabriel Borel he then formed a syndicate to produce aircraft in France. Unfortunately, this consortium was to be rather short-lived, disbanding

This Morane made a significant flight to Bizerta on 23 September 1913, piloted by factory flyer Roland Garros, later to win distinction as a military pilot in the First World War. The French firm of Morane, subsequently part of Morane-Saulnier, was an early specialist in monoplane construction. *(Bruce Robertson Collection)*

The Morane-Saulnier Type 'H' in early 1914. This aircraft design was soon to be used in numbers in the conflict which opened that August. *(Bruce Robertson Collection)*

The Borel floatplane design of 1913. Piloted by M. Clemet, this machine flew from Paris to Deauville on 24 August 1913. Borel, an early car manufacturer and friend of Wilbur Wright, later turned to aeroplane construction. *(Bruce Robertson Collection)*

in October of the year it was formed after the production of only a single monoplane. Borel subsequently continued his work on monoplanes producing a two-seater before turning to floatplanes and, in the 1920s, racing aircraft.

Reforming their organisation after the rift, the brothers took another partner, Raymond Saulnier who had recently won distinction as the designer of the Blériot XI monoplane, the machine used for the historic cross-Channel flight two years before. The new business partners specialised in the production of high-speed machines, again of monoplane configuration. The first of these were of the Parasol type, seeing service with the Aviation Corps at the outbreak of war in 1914, with Aéroplanes Morane-Saulnier, Soc. de Constructions Aéronautiques evolving into an influential manufacturer with headquarters at 205 Boulevard Pereire, Paris, and its own flying school at Villacoublay.

Léon Morane was to die in 1918, but the organisation continued under Robert until, two years before his own death in 1968, the firm of Morane-Saulnier ceased to exist in its original form, its name changing to Socata (a part of Sud) thus breaking France's final tie with the pioneering days of European aviation.

SEVEN

SKILL

What is chiefly needed is skill more than machinery.

Wilbur Wright, 1899

As the end of the first decade of the twentieth century loomed, for most of the Western world it became clear that two definitive periods of flying were over. The first was that of the amateur experimenter, followed by the age of the more scientific approach, the latter now giving way before the emergence of an entirely new industry, many of whose members had based their enterprises on the groundbreaking work of aviation's early pioneers.

A case in point was that of Louis Charles-Joseph Blériot. By 1909 he had nearly exhausted his fortune, amassed in the manufacture of high-quality motor-lamps, and it therefore came as a surprise when an offer of F25,000 enabled him to make the first successful crossing of the English Channel. However, this triumph was followed by so many injuries sustained in winning a number of other prizes, including one for speed, that he was forced to give up flying to concentrate his energies on business orders for copies of the Blériot XI. These began to pour in, so that earlier, somewhat rudimentary manufacturing methods had to be abandoned in favour of the first specially created and properly equipped factory for the production of flying machines in France. This enterprise delivered over eight hundred machines of forty different types between the time of its creation and August 1914, following which the output tempo was accelerated to produce an astonishing eighteen machines a day for the war effort. In addition to the factory, and like the Wrights before him, Blériot founded an accompanying flying school, at Buc. After the war, Blériot-Aéronautique combined with the Société pour Aviation et ses Derives (Société SPAD) in 1921 to form Blériot-SPAD, later becoming part of the Marcel Dassault organisation.

Louis Blériot died of a heart attack in 1936. A contemporary remembered him as 'a lovely gentleman, very warmhearted who took an interest, it seemed, in everybody', but perhaps his most enduring memorial is to be found in his famous Type XI monoplane. This machine sold in Britain at the time for £275 for the airframe alone, the final cost reaching £480 for those fitted with a 25-hp Anzani motor, or £580 if the power unit was a 30-hp Darracq. By July 1910, aircraft of this design held the duration record at 5 hours 3 minutes 5 seconds, and by 1911, that for distance – some 393¾ miles. By March 1913 the altitude record had been progressively raised by Gnome-powered Blériots of 50, 70, or ultimately 80-hp models to 19,290 feet, while the speed record was secured twice, at 47¾ mph on 28 August 1909 in a machine powered by a 60-hp ENV motor and finally on 29 October in the following year to 67½ mph in a Blériot powered by a 100-hp Gnome.

The monocoque construction of aircraft, whereby the main loads are taken by the fuselage or nacelle skin, was popularised in a strange way, resulting from the appeal of sales entrepreneur Armand Deperdussin for a dummy aeroplane to be exhibited in 1909 outside a Paris department store to advertise its goods. The result, constructed by Louis Bechereau, was potentially so good that Armand proposed the formation of an aircraft construction company with Louis as chief designer, employing the monocoque method which had first been suggested by the Swiss Eugène Ruchonnet.

The result of the new enterprise was a shoulder-wing monoplane with an extremely shallow fuselage, powered by a 70-hp Austro-Daimler motor. In 1910 production was begun of the first of the racers for which the company was to become famous; like all Deperdussin machines, it was fitted with wing-warping and powered by a 50-hp Gnome. This was followed by a two-seat reconnaissance machine with either an 80-hp Anzani or 100-hp

A Blériot aviation advertisement with a monkey-like creature pointing to the company name which extends from its tail. Louis Blériot financed his aeronautical ambitions with the profits from the sale of his superb acetylene car lamps, one of which remains on this advertisement. (*Author's collection*)

Blériot XI monoplane used by Adolphe Pegoud, and with which he became the first man to make sustained, inverted flight on 21 September 1913. *(Bruce Robertson Collection)*

Climbing away from Melbourne with the first air mail for Sydney, the Blériot monoplane used by Maurice Guillaux makes a dramatic picture. *(V.J. Garwood Collection)*

ndley Page E. H.P.5 of 1911. This resembled the earlier 'Yellow Peril' largely because it had the similar Weiss wing-form, at the time described as being of 'scimitar shape'. The
ne was sometimes known as 'The Blue Bird' from its fuselage and tailplane being that colour with a white, rubberised covering elsewhere. It first flew on 26 April 1912. *(Bruce
'son Collection)*

Gnome and, in 1912, by a three-seater with a span of 43 feet together with a small school machine with a 35-hp Anzani in 1913. It was while testing one of these models, which had been brought to England, that Geoffrey de Havilland claimed a maximum speed of 47⅓ mph after climbing to an altitude of 1,000 feet in 8 minutes.

In 1913 the name Deperdussin was associated with successful racing machines and Deperdussin was at the pinnacle of his reputation, only to be arrested for fraud. This débâcle forced him to sell the business to Louis Blériot. Four years of complex litigation ended with Armand being convicted and given a suspended sentence, but he was now almost bankrupt and in 1924 he shot himself.

Born in Cheltenham in 1885 and a qualified electrical engineer, Frederick Handley Page became interested in aviation while still a 21-year-old product designer for a large electrical manufacturing company. He formed a friendship with Alsace-born artist Jose Weiss, the pair making a series of flying models to

Jose Weiss showed this improved version of his 1905 glider in Paris, patenting the design three years later. In 1910 he adapted it for an experimental powered version. *(Bruce Robertson Collection)*

widen their knowledge of aerodynamics. By 1908, Handley Page felt that he had gained sufficient experience to branch out into the man-carrying field with the result that, like the Wrights, he embarked on gliding as a step towards powered flight, the influence of Weiss being reflected in the crescent shape of the wings which he regarded as ensuring automatic stability, a conviction based on trials with over two hundred miniature gliders. The device was fitted with a tricycle undercarriage and was flown from the top of a dyke in order to assist take-off.

In the following year their accumulated knowledge was applied to a machine powered by a 25-hp, four-cylinder air-cooled motor, the covering of the 32 foot 6 inch wings and fuselage being a blue-grey rubberised fabric which soon earned the machine the name of 'Bluebird'. An unusual feature of the type was fitting the wheels on short axles at each end of a lateral, ash leaf-spring so that the undercarriage presented a somewhat alarming appearance. Alas, it was not entirely successful, being seriously underpowered and capable of only a few hops when it was tested on 26 May 1910. Nevertheless, it was followed by the rather better H.P.3 model which was exhibited at the Olympia Aero Show in 1910, the similar H.P.4, popularly known as the 'Antiseptic' or 'Yellow Peril' from the colour of its dope, shown at the next Olympia show of 1911, while the same venue was to feature the first entirely successful Handley Page, the H.P.5, in 1913 after tests at Hendon during the previous year. The two-seat H.P.6 followed, intended for the Military Trials, but although reasonably successful, winning an Admiralty order, it crashed on 15 December 1912, killing both occupants.

A series of strange-looking biplanes came next, culminating in the H.P.8, a two-seater intended for an attempt at an Atlantic crossing, for which the *Daily Mail* offered a £10,000 prize to the winner. But the H.P.8 was never completed due to the outbreak of war in 1914, at which point the Handley Page firm began specialising in weight-lifting aircraft. Production of this type was to continue into the post-war world.

Jose Weiss had financed his early trials with miniature gliders from the ready sales which his paintings attracted. Born to a wealthy father in France in 1859, he later settled in England where he read several papers on the advantages of crescent wings to the British (later Royal) Aeronautical Society in 1907 and 1908, for which his earlier studies of science and engineering at Lille rendered him well qualified. The site of his first full-size glider trials in 1909 – his model differed from that of Handley Page and was named 'Olive' after one of his five daughters – was near Arundel Castle in Sussex. It was later fitted with a J.A.P. (James A. Prestwick) motor and then with an Anzani, both without success. The succeeding Pusher Monoplane Powered Glider *Madge* and Tractor

The beautiful Lavasseur-designed Antoinette IV monoplane shows its lines over spectators at an early air meeting. *(Author's collection)*

Another view of a different Antoinette monoplane said to be flown by Hubert Latham, a Blériot rival for the English Channel crossing, as shown on a postcard of 1909. *(Author's collection)*

Latham makes a low pass in the angular yet beautiful Antoinette type. *(Author's collection)*

Monoplane *Elsie* were no more successful; *Sylvia*, however, did prove a success until destroyed in an emergency landing on a sewage farm near Brooklands on 22 December 1910.

Meanwhile, it was realised that progress in the aircraft industry was inextricably linked to advances in the provision of lightweight petrol engines. Léon Lavasseur proved a virtuoso in this field, being encouraged by government grant in 1903 to build an aeroplane. Duly completed, this was wheeled out for trials overnight at Puteaux only to prove a failure; although another was built, it was never tested. Henceforth, Lavasseur turned his attention to aero-engines. In this he was encouraged by Jules Gastambide, after whose beautiful daughter, Antoinette, Léon named his first motor, a remarkably advanced piece of engineering with evaporation cooling, fuel injection and a construction from aluminium alloys to conserve weight. In 1906 the two men combined with Louis Blériot to market this motor, which was available in 24-hp and 50-hp versions.

By the following year, Blériot felt that his position as a director of an organisation likely to compete with his own was untenable, Léon's own interest in aircraft design having been reawakened, so Blériot resigned. Lavasseur produced another unsuccessful aeroplane, the Gastambide-Mengin I, a monoplane distinguished by a huge dihedral. Even so, he refused to be discouraged and resolutely went ahead, eliminating the faults and improving the design which was to re-emerge later in 1908 as the 'Antoinette IV', probably one of the most gracefully beautiful aeroplanes in the history of flight.

Unfortunately, despite its appearance in 1911, the 'Monoblock' failed to eclipse the popularity of the previous type, which retained its prime position even after Hubert Latham was forced to land one in the water in a failed bid to beat Blériot's cross-Channel record of 1909. But as aircraft design advanced, competition damaged the fortunes of the company so that Lavasseur, who died in 1922, was then on the brink of bankruptcy.

When interest in aerial travel was still centred on balloons, two who had a small corner in their production in the early 1900s were Albert Eustace Short and his younger brother Hugh Oswald Short. In 1908, the pair were joined by the third brother, Horace Leonard Short, when it was decided to begin the production of aeroplanes. The following year they received an order worth £8,400 for six Wright biplanes, Horace travelling to France to measure up a genuine example in order to expedite their construction. But to meet this order on their own, work on the Short No. 1 for F.K. McClean at Battersea had to be suspended, work in the meantime having begun on a Short-Wright glider. This was successfully flown by Alec Ogilvie and C.S. Rolls, three of the six powered machines going to these latter gentlemen, Rolls using his to make the first ever non-stop return flight across the English Channel on 2 June 1910. Earlier Rolls had described the experience of flight as 'a fresh gift from the Creator, the greatest treasure yet given to man', so impressed had he been by a flight in company with Wilbur Wright during 1908.

In August of the previous year, the Shorts had also produced their Short No. 2 which clearly owed something to Wright inspiration. J.T.C. Moore Brabazon used this model to win the £1,000 offered by the *Daily Mail* for the first all-British circular flight of 1 mile at Shellbeach, Isle of Sheppey, on 30 October 1909. This machine was subsequently modified in 1910 to become the Short No. 3. Three further aircraft appeared in swift succession, all owing something to Farman designs in their appearance. Two monoplanes followed, one a tractor, the other a pusher.

By 1914, an additional thirteen designs had been produced by the Short factory, many of these planes being capable of operating from water, so initiating the trend for the firm to concentrate on such aircraft that would last for the next twenty years. Probably the most interesting of the early examples was the Short

The Roe 1 triplane of 1909. *(Bruce Robertson Collection)*

Folder Seaplane of 1913 which introduced hinged wings to facilitate stowage and transportation, although fresh ground was clearly broken in the same year with the appearance of the S.81 Guncarrier which mounted at first a Vickers 1-pounder and then, two years later, a Davis 6-pound gun with success.

Edwin Alliot Verdon Roe, the son of a Manchester doctor, followed a chequered career from the age of fourteen, first in Canada as a forester, fisherman and surveyor, then returning to England as an apprentice on the railway, in a boat-yard and finally qualifying as a marine engineer at London University. In his spare time he won renown as a champion in the cycle craze currently sweeping the civilised world. Later he became interested in aviation as a consequence of a brief stay in the United States where he assisted in the construction of an experimental helicopter before 1907. The interest in aeronautics that this stimulated revealed itself in the series of experiments with models he conducted after returning home, when he took brief employment as an automobile draughtsman. It was during this period that he wrote to Wilbur Wright telling him of his ambitions, and was both surprised and encouraged to receive a sympathetic and helpful reply.

It is said that he used the prize money won by one of the 8-foot models to finance construction of a scaled-up version which, fitted with a 9-hp J.A.P. motor, proved underpowered. Later powered by a 24-hp Antoinette motor and fitted with additional, mid-fuselage lifting surfaces, towed off by a car it managed to fly in June 1908.

'The Bullseye' was a more conventional-looking triplane that was completed with help from Humphrey Roe in the railway-arch workshop at Lea Marshes, Hackney, where it was successfully flown in 1909. There followed the Avros 2 and 3 – a twin-seater – before the more ambitious No. 4 whose appearance was to herald that of three biplanes. These were in turn followed by a cabin monoplane in 1911, the year after the foundation of A.V. Roe and Co. (AVRO) which company was to construct over eight hundred versions of the legendary Avro 504 during the First World War.

News of the Wright brothers' success at Kitty Hawk captured the imagination of 21-year-old Geoffrey de Havilland and he experienced an overwhelming desire to fly even though he was at that point involved in the business of road transport. He designed a successful motorcycle engine before leaving Crystal Palace Engineering School and joining the staff of Willans & Robinson, manufacturers of turbines, steam and gas engines.

The son of the rector of Crux Easton, Hampshire, and fortunate in having received £1,000 from his grandfather, Geoffrey began to remedy a perceived

Work in progress on the 'Avroplane' beside the railway arches at Lea Green, 5 June 1909. *(Bruce Robertson Collection)*

gap in the market for a suitable aero-engine. He settled down to design one, the result being a 50-hp, water-cooled, four-cylinder, horizontally opposed motor weighing 250 lb, drawings for which he submitted to the Iris Motor Company of Willesden which agreed to produce a prototype for £250.

At this juncture he and his friend Frank Hearle decided to build an aeroplane around an engine of which they expected to take delivery six months later. The aeroplane turned out to have a wingspan of 36 feet with inverse-tapered ailerons and a wire-braced, whitewood open-girder fuselage, 29 feet long, its motor, mounted behind the pilot's seat, transmitting power to the two adjustable-pitch, aluminium pusher propellers.

Taken to de Havilland's Hampshire home in April, the plane was not in fact tested until a bright afternoon in December 1909. A helpful breeze blowing up

The de Havilland 1 which was constructed in a shed at Fulham, South London, between 1908 and 1909. The delay was caused by the search for a suitable engine which drove twin propellers through shafts and gears, not chains as used by the Wrights. *(Author's collection)*

Geoffrey de Havilland seated at the controls of his de Havilland 2 some time in mid-September 1910. A former London bus designer, he is seen here with his friend and brother-in-law Frank Hearle, motor engineer, about to swing the airscrew behind. *(Bruce Robertson Collection)*

Blackburn Mercury monoplane powered by a 50-hp Gnome undergoing trials in the sands at Filey in 1911. Although the Wrights had tended to make biplanes popular, some favoured the monoplane. *(Bruce Robertson Collection)*

the hill ensured a flight of some 35 yards before first the port wing collapsed and then the starboard. In the ensuing crash Geoffrey suffered only minor injury, immediately ordering that the motor be salvaged for use in his next machine. All this was the almost direct result of his having been taken aloft by Wilbur Wright in the previous year, an event of which he was to comment that it was 'a turning point' in his life.

This aircraft was again a pusher resembling a Farman; taken for testing first to Lichfield in Hampshire and then to Newbury in Buckinghamshire, it behaved perfectly when flight was attempted on 10 September 1910. When Geoffrey de Havilland was offered employment by the Royal Aircraft Factory, that December, his de Havilland 2 machine was purchased for £400. Later, when a vacancy for a chief designer occurred with George Holt Thomas's Aircraft Manufacturing Company (Airco) at Hendon in 1914, de Havilland

Breguet biplane of 1913. With its novel four-wheel undercarriage it gave the appearance of being clumsy, but was in fact an efficient and sturdy design. *(Bruce Robertson Collection)*

was offered the post, gathering a team around him that included his friend of earlier days, F.T. Hearle.

Even before the French Revolution, the name of Breguet was well known for its wealth and connections with the royal court resulting from the family's position as clock-makers to the monarchy. A typical example of their enterprising spirit, Louis Breguet, born into that illustrious Parisian family in 1880, was to show himself possessed of their traditional business acumen. When he left the family firm in preference for a career in aviation in 1907, it was a move he was well qualified to make. He had displayed his innate technical skills by graduating from the Ecole Supérieure d'Electricité de Paris shortly before, the first flying machine with which he was involved being a notoriously unstable helicopter built by his brother Jacques and one Professor Charles Richet.

Louis's own aeroplane had to wait until June 1909 before it could be tested, the trials quickly vindicating its design; critics of its steel tube construction were confounded when it flew successfully that month. Unfortunately, the early promise of these trials was not confirmed by the tests at Rheims during the

The first of the Breguet series, this 1910 design was widely known as the 'Coffee Pot'. It achieved its claim to fame in August of the same year when it proved to have a stability unrivalled by any of its contemporaries. *(Author's collection)*

subsequent August. Louis Breguet, however, faced the official verdict with equanimity, going on in the following year to design an improved variant which was quickly dubbed the 'Coffee Pot' owing to its aluminium covering.

Since the designer was operating as little more than a lone gifted amateur at the time, it came as something of a surprise when, during 1911, he floated his own company, the Société Anonyme des Ateliers d'Aviation. Spurred on by the spectacle of eleven passengers being carried a distance of $3\frac{1}{10}$ miles over Douai in a 'massive aircraft' on 23 March that year, two years later there appeared his big four-float hydro-biplane which won the Grand Prix in a gale at Monaco in March 1913. Large numbers of his sturdy aircraft saw service during the First World War. Nine years before his death in 1955, Louis Breguet returned to the subject of his early investigations, building a twin-rotor helicopter which some consider the first such device to fly successfully.

When the modified Sopwith Tabloid floatplane (the changes were in the main to enable a larger-diameter rotary engine to be fitted) won the Schneider Trophy for Great Britain in 1914, it represented a success by a new aircraft building enterprise. The firm had been established in an abandoned roller-skating rink at Kingston-on-Thames by Thomas Octavius

Murdoch Sopwith, the son of wealthy parents who had trained as a civil engineer. In 1910 he purchased a Howard Wright monoplane (no connection with the Wright brothers) on which he promptly taught himself to fly, only to crash, replace the aircraft and try again. He gained Royal Aero Club Certificate No. 31 on 22 November 1910 and became an exhibition pilot, in December that year winning first prize for a long-distance flight from Eastchurch to Thirlmont in Belgium. Later he visited the United States where he astonished spectators by his skill and daring, at the same time carrying off a number of valuable prizes.

Returning to Great Britain, he founded the company that was to bear his name, gathering around himself the best experts available in the various branches of aeronautics. But he was careful to ensure that the firm did not become over-ambitious too soon. Its first aircraft were a Sopwith-modified Burgess-Wright biplane, originally purchased in America, followed by a

Four-float hydro-biplane, as it was known, of 1913, when it distinguished itself at Monaco. A type which owed much to the earlier Breguet landplane, it was powered by a 200-hp Samson engine and had inversely tapered ailerons. *(Author's collection)*

Thomas Sopwith, founder of a dynasty of British aeroplanes, beside the Howard Wright biplane in which he won the British Endurance Record on 10 December 1910. Two years later the company was to be joined by former schoolmaster R.J. Ashfield as chief designer. Ashfield became project engineer in 1914 when Herbert Smith became senior designer. *(Sopwith via Bruce Robertson)*

Sopwith-Wright biplane which had a covered fuselage and a tractor airscrew driven by a 70-hp Gnome rotary from a Blériot until November 1913 when it was replaced by an 80-hp Gnome.

After manufacturing a large number of differing aircraft during the First World War, including the fractious Sopwith F.1 and 2F.1 Camels, the firm went into voluntary liquidation soon after the Armistice. Reconstituted, it emerged as the Hawker Engineering Company in 1920–2, 'Tommy' Sopwith remaining chairman until 1963 when he was seventy-five years of age. He was to live on into his one hundred-and-first year, genial, hard-working and still possessed of a sharp mind with a brilliant and accurate recall of the rich cavalcade of aviation history which he had witnessed.

Many of these experimenters, pioneers and other enthusiasts had gathered in France in 1909 to take part in a 'Grande Semaine d'Aviation' at Rheims during the week beginning 22 August, a week in which, although Wilbur and Orville did not participate in person, the results of their efforts were nevertheless vindicated, beginning with a representation of a Wright-like aeroplane on the posters, followed by a fair number of successes achieved by Wright machines in the events, as shown by the table on p. 138.

The peak of early Sopwith achievement came in 1914 when Howard Pixon, flying this floatplane based on the 'Tabloid' design but modified to take a larger motor, won the Schneider Trophy for Britain. *(Author's collection)*

A Bristol Box-kite being demonstrated. On 15 November 1910 the first British contract was signed between the Russian military attaché in Paris and the British & Colonial Aeroplane Company for the supply of eight Bristol Box-kites. *(British Aerospace/Bruce Robertson Collection)*

GRAND PRIX DE CHAMPAGNE (for the longest distance flown)

	Pilot	Aircraft	Distance	Prize
1.	Farman	Farman biplane	112 miles	£2,000
2.	Latham	Antoinette monoplane	96½ miles	£1,000
3.	Paulan	Voisin biplane	82 miles	£400
4.	De Lambert	Wright biplane	72½ miles	£200
5.	Latham	Antoinette monoplane*	68 miles	£200
6.	Tissandier	Wright biplane	66 miles	£200

GORDON BENNETT CUP (for fastest time over 12½ miles)

	Pilot	Aircraft	Prize
1.	Glen Curtiss	Curtiss biplane	£1,000

PRIX DES PASSAGERS (for greatest number of passengers on one circuit)

	Pilot	Aircraft	No. of Passengers	Prize
1.	Farman	Farman biplane	Two passengers for 10 min 39 sec	£400

Prix de l'Altitude (for greatest height over 160 feet)

	Pilot	Aircraft	Height	Prize
1.	Latham	Antoinette monoplane	500 feet	£400

PRIX DE LA VITESSE (for highest speed over 18½ miles)

	Pilot	Aircraft	Speed	Prize
1.	Glen Curtiss	Curtiss biplane	26 min 40 sec	£400
2.	Tissandier	Wright biplane	28 min 59 sec	£200
3.	Lefebvre	Wright biplane	29 min	£120
4.	De Lambert	Wright biplane	29 min 2 sec	£80

(Prizes are expressed in the financial values of the time.)

* This was achieved in a second machine, and not that used for a distance flight at the same event.

The Bristol organisation was by no means wedded to the biplane concept, however, producing this Prier monoplane design in 1911. This example was to fly with No. 3 Squadron of the fledgling Royal Flying Corps after delivery at the beginning of 1912. *(Author's collection)*

Almost forgotten among the United States' pioneer flyers were the English-born Thomas brothers, one of their earliest types being the 1912 Thomas Morse TA, seen here with designer B.D. Morse (no relation) standing in front. The factory went on to produce the Thomas Morse S-4B and S-4C scouts of 1917/18.
(Bruce Robertson Collection)

These successes with Wright machines seemed to justify the US government's decision of February 1908, no doubt taken in the light of Wilbur's 24-mile flight of October 1905, to enter into a contract for a similar machine. Such a decision could have been made by Britain in 1904 when Colonel Capper, one of the country's few champions of flying at the time, having attended the St Louis exhibition to see if it contained anything likely to interest the War Office, unofficially visited Chanute, Langley and the Wrights. He found the latter on the point of closing down the Dayton station for the winter, the place in which they would construct a new machine based on the experience gained during that summer. Having satisfied himself of the brothers' honesty, Capper informally requested their terms for working in England. Their reply suggested that an acceptable sum would be £20,000 over a period of four years, although their own country would not to be excluded.

On his return home, Capper strongly advocated that the relevant government authorities explore the matter further. The lengthy correspondence which followed seemed to indicate agreement to supply a single machine and an instructor to fly it, when in December 1906 negotiations were officially terminated. A tentative fresh approach by the Wrights, apparently in a wish to reopen discussions, came to nothing. After a similar period of cold disinterest, the US government executed a sharp U-turn and signed the 1908 agreement, a decision which left Capper feeling that a more vigorous approach from the War Office would have placed Britain in a commanding position in the stressful years that were to come.

Eight

Warplanes

*When my brother and I built and flew the first man-carrying machine,
we thought that we were introducing into the world an invention
which would make further wars practically impossible.*

Orville Wright, 1917

Aware that they had evolved a device of enormous military potential, a
little less than a year after their success at Kitty Hawk the Wrights
decided to offer their design for a flying machine to the United States
Army, the historic proposal being made on 6 October 1905. Despite the fact
that they were flush from a fresh success – a new version of their biplane had
flown a distance of a little over 24 miles in a time of 38 minutes and 3 seconds
– one feels that Wilbur may have guessed the heading under which any such
proposal would be pigeon-holed; he concluded a letter to the Smithsonian
Institution in 1899 with the words 'I am an enthusiast, not a crank'.

That Wilbur had judged the official attitude correctly was proved by the
response the two men received. Dated 24 October, eighteen days after the
brothers' submission, the Board of Ordnance and Fortification stated that it 'does
not care to formulate any requirements for the performance of a flying machine
or take any action on the subject until a machine is produced which by actual
operation is shown to be able to produce horizontal flight and carry an operator'.

Nevertheless, attitudes to manned flight were rapidly changing. Only
two years later, on 1 August 1907, Brigadier General James Allen, commanding
officer of the United States Signal Corps, signed a confidential War Department
directive establishing an Aeronautical Division of the corps. This was the first
military organisation for heavier-than-air machines in the world, with
responsibility for 'balloons, air machines and kindred subjects'. A mere
four months later, on 23 December, the same Chief Signal Officer issued a
specification for a military aeroplane – the first such ever to seek commercial
tender. Its main requirements were that 'The machine should be quick and easy

A largely forgotten pioneer is Roger Sommer. The son of a wealthy French felt manufacturer, he learned to fly on a Farman aircraft which he purchased in 1909. During that year too, he took Gertrude Bacon aloft, the first Englishwoman to fly in a powered aircraft, and began constructing this aeroplane. Of his own design, it was to prove so successful that he went on to found an aircraft factory in his home town of Mouzon and a flying school at Douzy. *(Author's collection)*

to assemble and should be able to be taken apart and packed for transportation'; that it 'must be designed to carry two persons having a combined weight of about 350 lb and sufficient fuel for a flight of 125 miles'; and that it 'should be designed to have a speed of at least 40 miles per hour in still air'; finally, it had to 'be easily transportable on an Army waggon'. In addition, the specification demanded that such a military flying machine must be 'designed to ascend in any country which may be encountered in field service' and be able 'to land in a field without requiring a specially prepared spot, and without damaging its structure', while being 'sufficiently simple in its construction and operation to permit an intelligent man to become proficient in its use within a reasonable length of time'. Small wonder that on 6 February 1908 the US Army accepted a tender from the Wrights dated 2 February, to build a military flying machine for two occupants at a cost of $25,000. The contract was signed four days later, together with those submitted by a J. Scott and Augustus

A Wright Military Flyer, used as a demonstration machine during the US Signal Corps trials, in the process of being manhandled into its shed sometime before 1910. The work is watched by an officer, identified by his sword, who is in conversation with a straw-hatted civilian while three others, one a lady, watch on the right. *(USAF via Bruce Robertson)*

M. Herring, the same man who had visited the Wrights on several occasions at Kitty Hawk, immediately earning their distrust. In fact, the brothers' was the only machine to materialise.

Perhaps because Wilbur Wright had taken a lady passenger aloft in a two-seat version of the original biplane in the same year, the new machine, designed to meet the requirements of the Army, excited no great comment when it was delivered for official trials. These were successfully completed by 17 September 1908, with accompanying flight demonstrations at the parade ground at Fort Meyer, Virginia, just outside Washington. The machine was a two-seat version of the standard Wright Model 'A', having a wingspan of 36 feet 4 inches, a length of 28 feet and a gross weight of 1,200 lb, with 740 lb tare, capable of a maximum speed of 44 mph. The machine's construction earned the Wright brothers a bonus since its capacity exceeded requirements; indeed, penalty clauses had been appended to the contract in case of failure to meet the specifications.

A Military Wright Type 'A' in flight. *(USAF)*

The achievement of better-than-expected performance is interesting when it is realised that the Wright biplane was something of a dead-end design, its development potential severely limited. Such a shortcoming robbed Wilbur and Orville of any future monopoly with the result that this period, only three years after their historic first flight, was largely given over by the pair to retention of certain design fundamentals which they regarded as their own property, being the results of their own experimentation programme.

However, just as everything seemed to be going well with the world's first military example of their genius, tragedy struck unexpectedly on 17 September.

San Francisco-born Lieutenant Thomas E. Selfridge was a West Point military academy graduate and practical aviation enthusiast. Having introduced himself to Alexander Graham Bell, who in 1907 was forming a scientific association to investigate heavier-than-air flight following vague reports of the Wrights' success, Bell took on Selfridge as his assistant. Selfridge turned up at the trials of the Wright military biplane as a newly appointed officer of the Signal Corps, asking for a flight in the new machine.

This request put Orville in a difficult position. He had met the lieutenant in Washington during the summer and he believed that he was being pumped for information. Consequently he distrusted the younger man, but found it impossible to refuse the request in light of the 26-year-old lieutenant's official position. It was thus agreed that Orville would take him up on 17 September, when it was planned to test the pusher propellers that had been fitted, these having a diameter that had been increased by several inches.

The take-off was normal and a series of circular flights over the field was carried out at an altitude of only about 125 feet. Three had been completed and Orville was about to commence a fourth when he heard an unfamiliar tapping note from the rear of the machine. A hurried glance aft indicated nothing amiss but, as a precaution, he shut down the motor and prepared to land, believing that the sound was perhaps coming from the chain drives. Almost immediately two deep thumps were audible, the aircraft simultaneously swinging to the right. Since a gulley full of small trees lay directly ahead, Orville attempted to turn to the left and land on the Fort Meyer parade ground, only to find that the rudders were inoperative. He managed the turn partially by warping the wings alone, losing some 40 feet in altitude. Hardly had this manoeuvre commenced than the machine suddenly began to lose more height, at the same time refusing to straighten up. At an altitude of now no more than a negligible 25 feet, the machine showed signs of responding to the controls, but it was too late and it crashed heavily.

A crowd of bystanders rushed forward, led by Major George O. Squier, the Acting Chief Signals Officer and an army sergeant. They found Selfridge unconscious, his skull fractured from being thrown violently against one of the wing struts, an injury from which he died a few hours later. Orville sustained a broken left leg and four broken ribs, but it was not until twenty years later that three fractures of the hip bones, one dislocated, were finally discovered as a result of examination following his complaints of severe pain. It was while Orville was recuperating from the first of these diagnosed injuries that he gave his opinion as to the cause of the mishap after scrutinising pieces of the wrecked aircraft that were brought to his bedside.

The fault lay in the enlarged propellers. The one on the right had developed a crack, allowing the blade to flatten, the unequal thrust which resulted simultaneously setting up vibration so that the propeller swung sideways and fouled a wire to the tail; this in turn broke away and assumed a near horizontal position, lifting the rear of the machine in the process. Thus ended in tragedy the year that had dawned with so much promise when the Wrights had resumed flying on 6 May after a three-year abstinence. On 14 May, Wilbur had taken up Charles W. Furnas, arguably the world's first air passenger, for a 28-second flight, Orville taking him a distance of 2 miles later the same morning.

Meanwhile, the after-effects of the crash in which Selfridge had lost his life appeared to presage the end of the Army's brief flirtation with flying machines. The older, more traditionally minded senior officers were strongly opposed to the idea of continuing such trials, an attitude that may well have prevailed were it not for the strength of opinion of a small, far-sighted group of younger men of the Signal Corps. So vigorously did the latter insist that this sad occurrence must mark the beginning of fresh excursions into the unknown rather than the end, that they carried the day. A legend persists even now that it was because this small but vocal group pressed their case so persuasively, demanding that a machine must be ordered without delay for use in Signal Corps trials, that delivery of one was taken in July 1910. Thus it was that soon after, the US War Department was able to declare the country's air strength as: 'one officer, nine enlisted men, one Wright "aeroplane", one Baldwin airship and three captive balloons'. How shrewd was the judgement of these younger officers was to be proved three years later when, for

In June 1912 the first United States' trials calling for a machine-gun to be fired from an aircraft in flight are made from a Wright Type 'B' by Captain Charles de Forest Chandler seen here on the left. Lieutenant Thomas de Witt Milling acted as pilot but was unavailable for this photograph and replaced by a substitute. *(USAF)*

the expenditure of $435,000 over that period, a force of twenty-eight aeroplanes had been built up, some airworthy, some grounded, some good, others useless.

The year following the Fort Meyer crash seemed to augur better fortune: not only did the Department of Congress announce in March a grant of $125,000 for 'air operations in the fiscal year of 1912', but on 2 August 1910 the US Army announced the beginning of renewed trials with the fresh Wright machine specifically to 'determine the suitability of heavier-than-air craft for war purposes'. This aircraft, the world's first warplane, was a Type 'B', an improvement on the earlier Type 'A', from which it differed chiefly in having the forward elevators now transferred aft, although retaining the two-lever controls but with the landing skids now supported on wheels. To this machine (serial No. 3) was soon added a second Type 'B' (serial No. 4), the pair being used for training, with pupil and instructor sharing the same set of controls. Interestingly, these were only partially duplicated, the arrangement on the first Wright biplanes being preserved in principle, so that the elevators were operated by a lever on the pilot's left, the wing-warp being activated by that on the right, a small auxiliary lever on the top of this moving the rudders.

This pair of 'B' models (a variant introduced in 1911) would be augmented some time later by an order for no less than seven of the new Wright Type 'C' biplanes that were to be awarded military serial numbers (7, 8 and 10 to 14 inclusive). Although of virtually the same design as the preceding Type 'B's, they differed in being powered at first by a 22/27-hp Barringuard motor – a Wright design; at least one model was later fitted with a 55-hp motor, sometimes referred to as 'a 60-hp Wright'. This also varied from the previous 'B' model in having full dual controls, some of these machines also replacing the levers by twin wheels mounted on a single yoke.

Eight years after Wilbur and Orville's historic first flight, not only the Americans but also Europeans were realising the potential of the new ability to fly. In Europe, the French took the lead, attaching a Wright biplane to the 2nd Corps for the 1912 manoeuvres in September. Its acquisition was the direct result of a military mission to the Wrights six years before, its brief to obtain a manufacturing licence for the type, and although this was not forthcoming for another two years, by August 1909, General Roques was about to order a pair of Wright biplanes.

Meanwhile, the US Navy had not remained unaware of the service potential of the new form of locomotion and as a result purchased three Type 'C-H' machines ('hydro' or seaplane versions of the Type 'C'), their first designations being B-1, B-2 and B-3 (later to be reclassified as AH-4, AH-5 and AH-6). These were flown by the Navy as either land- or seaplane forms, the latter with three-step floats, the former achieving a marginally better performance.

During the years immediately preceding the outbreak of the First World War, the Wright foundation had taken the obvious step of establishing a flying school where tuition might be had in the handling of the flying machines. Many of the pupils went on indirectly to further the cause of the use of Wright

General 'Hap' Arnold, as a West Point cadet, at the Wrights' Dayton school early in 1911. He would raise the army altitude record to 6,450 feet during the following year. *(USAF)*

machines for military purposes, although the thinking of the time had so far failed to appreciate that their development potential was limited, if only because the design was inherently unstable in the lateral plane. However, many of the pilots who were later to go to war in better machines were originally students of the Wright school at Simms Station, Dayton, Ohio. Among those who were later to enjoy fame was 25-year-old Henry Harley Arnold. He had graduated from West Point in 1907 and after a spell of service in the Philippines transferred to the Signal Corps in 1911, immediately taking pilot instruction from Orville Wright himself.

A course at the Wright school was usually of about three hours duration and this, later recalled by 'Hap', as Arnold subsequently became known, included tuition on a 'simulator' mounted on a sawhorse that was used during gaps in the actual air instruction. Actual flight was always dependent on the prevailing weather so that each time in the air seldom lasted more than 10 or 15 minutes. But despite frustrations such as these, after an accumulated instruction time of some 3 hours and 48 minutes, Arnold was duly qualified as a pilot and awarded Aviator's Certificate No. 29. In November of the following year, he flew from Fort Riley, Kansas to make the first artillery observations from a Wright 'C' powered by a 55-hp motor and transmitting the results to the ground by use of an early one-way radio, a flight on which he was accompanied by Lieutenant A.L.P. Sands of the Field Artillery. In that year, too, Arnold set an altitude record of 6,450 feet before going on to organise an air command in the Panama Canal Zone during the First World War. He eventually became a member of the Joint Chiefs of Staff in the Second World War.

Military flights such as these were now slowly being accepted by even the most reactionary members of the 'Old Guard' among staff officers, a reluctant change of attitude no doubt brought about by the fact that in 1911 Europe had come very close to war. (In the late summer of that year the German Kaiser had sent the gunboat *Panther* to the Moroccan port at the mouth of the River Sus allegedly having promised to assist the natives in their struggle with France, so provoking what became known as the Agadir Crisis.)

But perhaps the foremost pupil of the Wright school was Englishman Griffith Brewer, who received instruction from Orville and qualified as a pilot with American Certificate No. 307 on 15 August 1914. He later went on to represent the Wright organisation as its British Empire Sales Manager in the dying years of peace, his name heading the list of twenty other British subjects holding American certification from the Wright school, several of whom saw war service. Their names are worth recording:

Certificate No.	Name	Date Qualified
335	J. Morrow Alexandra	22 July 1915
339	W.B. Evans	7 August 1915
343	Arthur Cyril Harland	7 September 1915
346	George H. Simpson	2 October 1915
347	Gordon Fraser Ross	6 October 1915
348	K.G. Macdonald	8 October 1915
349	Percy B. Beasley	8 October 1915
350	Stearne T. Edwards	11 October 1915
353	K.F. Saunders	19 October 1915
356	Murray Bayne Galbraith	3 November 1915
357	Arthur Gerald Woodward	5 November 1915
358	Walter James Sussan	9 November 1915
359	John Clark Simpson	9 November 1915
361	Arthur Roy Brown	13 November 1915
362	Lieutenant Harley G. Smith	17 November 1915
363	Cuthbert J. Creery	24 November 1915
364	John Galpin	24 November 1915
365	Basil D. Hobbs	2 December 1915
366	James Lindsay Gordon	2 December 1915
367	William Edgar Robinson	7 December 1915

Wright biplanes were used throughout for instructing and testing these pupils.

Even before these dates, the US military had, not unnaturally, begun to take an active interest in the possibility of using Wright aeroplanes for warlike purposes, the first of the associated trials being devoted to the issue of dropping bombs, a means of attack that had occupied men's minds since the days of the balloon. Hence, on 7 January 1911, the first test using a small hand-dropped high-explosive bomb was made by Lieutenant Crissy from the starboard seat of a Wright Type 'B' over San Francisco Bay with Lieutenant Parmelee beside him acting as pilot. So successful was this trial considered that a second, similar one was carried out on 15 January with the same crew – the first attempts to drop high-explosive missiles from an American aircraft.

Clearly, the military were now taking man's ability to fly more seriously, as indicated by a sortie, again using a Wright biplane, that was carried out the

The first trials calling for live bombs to be dropped from an American aircraft in flight are made over San Francisco Bay by Lieutenants Myron S. Crissy and Phillip O. Parmelee on 7 and 15 January 1911. A Wright Type 'B' is used. *(USAF)*

following day. This was the Army's first photographic reconnaissance mission and was successfully completed by G.E.M. Kelly and W. Brookins; the following year would witness trials intended to assertain whether it was possible to fire a machine-gun from an aircraft in flight.

This development had been anticipated using a 1903 Springfield rifle when, in August 1910, Major Jacob E. Fickle had taken one aloft in a Curtiss machine piloted by Charles F. Willard and from an altitude of only 100 feet fired two rounds at a target over Sheepshead Bay, New York. Although little was done to develop the idea of an airborne gunner beyond a flurry of attempts to

Wright Type 'F' at North Island. This type represented an attempt to substitute a fuselage for the original booms and move the entire empennage aft to convert the Wright for military use.
(Erikson Collection/USAF)

devise several recoilless guns, some more dangerous to the gunner than his target, it was not for another two years that thought was given to the use of a machine-gun from an aeroplane.

It was 2 June 1912 when Captain C. de F. Chandler, the commanding officer of the aviation section of the Signals Corp at College Park, Maryland, took off in a Wright Type 'B' biplane, the captain carrying a Lewis gun between his knees. Despite being himself a certificated pilot, holding qualification No. 59, on this occasion he was being flown by Lieutenant T. de Witt Milling, the holder of Certificate No. 30. The target set out in front of a hangar below consisted of nothing more elaborate than a rectangle of cheesecloth measuring 6 feet by 7 feet, which he succeeded in riddling with bullet holes from an altitude of 250 feet, before turning away and sending a blast of fire into some tempting fishponds for good measure.

That an interest in aviation was not confined to the higher echelons but was equally shared by the younger generation of serving officers must by now have

Another attempt to modernise the original Wright configuration for army use was made in 1910 resulting in the Wright Type 'HS', although on both improvements the chain-driven propellers were retained. *(Erikson Collection/USAF)*

become abundantly clear. The names of a small number have already been mentioned, but there were others who showed their early interest in Wright machines before going on to establish the unspectacular but necessary groundwork of a new type of fighting force. Among such men were Lieutenant Frank Purdy Lahm, the Ohio-born son of a balloon enthusiast who had his interest in powered flight stimulated by a trip with Orville Wright during a flying demonstration at Fort Meyer, Virginia, on 9 September 1908. The experience eventually made him the first US Army officer to go aloft in an aeroplane and, in 1909, one of the first two officers to be taught to fly by Orville; the greater part of Lahm's subsequent military career was spent in the founding of training stations.

Another enthusiast was Lieutenant (later Major-General) Benjamin D. Foulois who had enlisted in the Army at the age of nineteen, receiving a commission three years later. Having learned the art of flying a balloon in the basket of the first vehicle of that type used by the Army, in 1909 he began to train as a pilot under Orville Wright. The following year he flew solo in the

Army's first aeroplane at Fort Sam, Houston, before embarking on a career that was to culminate in his achieving the rank of major-general; later he would concentrate on the techniques of artillery observation and pioneering air to ground radio.

As it happens, the aircraft concerned is preserved to this day, not for its association with Foulois, but rather for its claim to historical significance. But Wright machines produced for military duties seemed to enjoy a surprising reputation for operational longevity, records existing of a much repaired, patched Wright Type 'B' that was still in use as a trainer at the Stinton school, San Antonio, in December 1915 when it was finally destroyed in a crash. Another Wright military plane has been described as being used for training at Dayton, Ohio, some months later, what is believed to have been its final use for a solo flight taking place on 3 July 1916. Military Wrights were comparatively common survivors in 1914, the US Army retaining a single Wright Type 'B', two Type 'C's and the same number of Type 'D's, the US Navy at the same time allegedly still operating 'one or more Wrights' – perhaps a reference to possible survivors of the 1912 purchase of the three Type 'C-H' machines.

Even in Czarist Russia, a very distant country in those days of slow communications, Wright machines were to be found, records existing of a Type 'R' in use there. This particular machine was referred to as a 'German Wright', since it incorporated significant modifications, although these were basically features of other type 'R's which included twin rudders aft of an all-moving horizontal tail, the canard foreplane now replaced by extended skids as a protection against nosing over after a bad landing. This Russian example was associated with the amazing skills of pilot V.M. Abramovich who was to meet a tragic death on 24 April 1913, in a crash while instructing Princess Schakovskaya. The Princess, who was at the controls at the time, escaped with only slight injuries. A Wright of earlier vintage is known to have been operated by the Gatchino Flying School in 1910.

The science of flight was advancing at a prodigious pace as the century advanced. However, aircraft procurement for military use became more cautious, for it was now realised that unlike the use of aircraft for warlike purposes – something which was now accepted – the Wright biplane design had no military potential, with the result that purchase of Wright Types 'EX' and 'E' was avoided. These models were nevertheless interesting enough, the former being little more than a single-seat version of the Type 'B', the latter basically a modified version of the Type 'EX' with a single pusher propeller.

Reservations aside, the US Army had shown some interest in the redesigned Type 'B'. This was to become known as the Model 'HS' on which the former open-girder rear booms were abandoned in favour of a conventional fuselage adopted to house the two-man crew and the 55-hp Wright engine, although this still drove twin propellers in the former manner, with the aid of chains. Wing-warping was also retained. Its span was 32 feet, the length 29 feet 6 inches and the all-up weight 1,000 lb; it is claimed to have been capable of a maximum speed of 70 mph. The Army operated this unique Wright machine from San Diego.

Another, somewhat similar machine from the Wright works which interested the Army, but was never adopted due to its disappointing performance, was that which for test purposes briefly enjoyed the military designation of Airplane 39. This was the Type 'F' which was supplied to the US Signal Corps on 29 June 1914. Promptly dubbed the 'Tin Cow', it had a similar layout to that of the 'HS' but was fitted with a 90-hp Austro-Daimler engine, although even this still powered the twin, pusher propellers through chain drive. A slightly larger aircraft than the 'HS', it had a wingspan of 42 feet and a length of 29 feet 6 inches. Capable of a claimed speed of 60 mph, it weighed 2,100 lb and was broken up on 14 June of the following year.

Britain also procured a Wright Type 'F'. This was powered by a 60-hp Wright motor, the first mention of it being dated 7 September 1915. Aside from the

The beginning of Philip O. Parmelee's distinguished career was to be marked by not only such pioneer work in connection with the United States' first attempts to drop bombs, but also the carriage of freight by air when he was asked to act as the pilot of a Wright Type 'B' to deliver several hundred yards of silk on behalf of the Home Dry Goods Store. *(Bruce Robertson Collection)*

fact that it never received a serial number and the belief that it was briefly flown with an enlarged radiator, details of its ultimate fate are lost.

The US Navy also continued to show an interest in Wright designs with the result that in 1914 a Type 'G', also known as the 'Aerobat', was tested under the identification of 'AH-19'. Unfortunately, its performance was to prove poor and it was rejected. More successful were the Type 'K' floatplanes which had also adopted conventional fuselage construction with rear empennages. New also was the introduction of tractor propellers, although these continued to be chain-driven, and ailerons had not yet replaced the wing-warping of the earlier types. Nevertheless only one such aircraft was ever co-opted into naval service, initially identified as 'AH-23', a designation later changed to 'A51' with the adoption of a new numbering scheme. In Italy Sezione Aviazione Maria similarly used a 'Wright Seaplane' as a military trainer on the firm's inception in early 1913, the machine surviving into the war years.

It was on 3 March 1910 that history had been made at Fort Sam Houston, San Antonio, Texas when Lieutenant Benjamin Foulois* took aloft a Wright Type 'A', so making the first flight by a military pilot at the controls of a military aircraft in the United States.

Meanwhile, production of Wright biplanes continued, their design and construction still following much the original concept as that of the machine which had changed the world at Kitty Hawk in December seven years earlier. However, only one year before the outbreak of the First World War it was announced that while the constructors hoped to complete machines numbered 1 to 10, plus several more currently building, to meet firm orders, 'most cannot be supplied until a new works has been erected'.

Indeed, 1916 was to prove something of a watershed for Orville Wright. Coping with increasing international demands alone now, since the death of Wilbur four years previously, he entered into a merger of his main business interests with the General Aeronautic Company, General Motors, the Glen L. Martin, the Simplex Automobile Company and Wright Flying Field Inc., the

---

* Holding the rank of captain by 1916, Foulois was in command of the 1st Aero Squadron, a unit which by May consisted of 16 officers (10 of them pilots), 122 enlisted men and 8 aircraft. These were sent to support Brigadier-General John Pershing's punitive expedition against Mexican insurgent leader Pancho Villa; it is recorded that while in charge of this expedition, Pershing flew on the first possible occasion to make a reconnaissance as observer to Captain Dodd in Curtiss JN4, No. 44.

An early Farman, seen in 1907. It differs from later variants mainly in having an open pilot's position, later to be replaced by a simple nacelle. It is powered by a Wolseley motor and is lettered 'Aeroplanes Voisin' on the tail curtain. *(Bruce Robertson Collection)*

consortium being known as the Wright-Martin Aircraft Corporation. At the time of the merger, the enterprise boasted 2,400 employees and a capital of $5,000,000, with a head office at 60 Broadway, New York City, a Western office at 937 S, Los Angeles Street, Los Angeles, California, and one for European business at 35 bis Rue d'Anjou, Paris. In addition, there were facilities at Los Angeles and at Hampstead Plains, Long Island, where there was also a factory, and a seaplane station at Port Washington. Other factories were based at New York and at the Simplex Works at New Brunswick. President of the new corporation was Edward H. Hagar, Glen L. Martin acting as vice-president together with C.S. Johnson, while the secretary was J.G. Dudley. Thereafter Orville was to continue as a private experimenter at the Dayton works.

It was only eleven years after the Wrights' first flight that war broke out in Europe, the United States not entering the conflict until three years later, in 1917. Although a small number of Wright-built machines existed, officially attached to the newly emergent military air arms, the extremely limited development potential of their design, coupled with the rapidity with which aeroplane design in general had advanced in the few intervening years once the age-old secret of mechanical flight had been unlocked, meant that no Wright machine of any type ever saw operational service.

Certainly, the French Army had taken delivery of its first flying machine in the form of a Wright biplane at Satory near Versailles on 10 February 1910, General Roques immediately launching a campaign to recruit pilots for the new arm. All of the volunteers answering this call were service men, four from the infantry and three from the artillery; perhaps not surprisingly none came from the cavalry, despite the now-accepted fact that the horseman's 'good hands' are little different from those required to fly an aeroplane with sensitivity. The first of these volunteers to receive his military pilot's brevet was Lieutenant Felix Camerman, who was subsequently promoted to command the Chalons military aviation school. However, even by this date the Wright biplane was regarded as obsolete, the first operational sortie of the new Aéronautique Militaire, made on 9 June of the same year, being one to take aerial photographs from a Blériot XI/2 crewed by Capitaine Marconnet and Lieutenant Fequant during a flight from Chalons to Vincennes.

The last recorded use of a Wright machine for military purposes was when one was attached to the 9th Corps in company with a pair of Farmans and a single Blériot during the September manoeuvres of 1910, and such was the success with which the aeroplanes met (two Henry Farmans, a Sommer and a Blériot XI/2 supporting the 2nd Corps) that General Roques was moved to order more aeroplanes, raising France's military potential in the air to 29 machines by the end of the year, the original total of 7 pilots having now risen to 39.

Great Britain's Royal Flying Corps, newly constituted one year later, had little use for the Wright design apart from that already outlined, although the single example recorded as 'old' in March 1911 was probably the same machine that was to be described as warped and obsolete a short time later. The War Office, however, did express its thanks to C.S. Rolls for placing his personal machine at its disposal if required early in 1910; a state of affairs no doubt due in part to the emergence of a vigorous aviation industry at home.

In America the situation was of course somewhat different, the US Signal Corps Aeronautical Division issuing its first Field Order on 5 March 1913 establishing the 1st Aero Squadron at Galveston Bay, Texas. This was commanded by none other than Captain Charles de F. Chandler, the same who had participated in the experiment calling for the firing of a Lewis gun from the Wright Type 'B' the year before – probably the same Wright that was still in service with the Signal Corps at the time of the foundation of the 1st Aero Squadron in 1913.

REQUIEM

We all give our lives to something – give them away.

C.S. Rolls, 1910

It was an early February day in 1948 and the minister was conducting a funeral that he knew would become a part of history, one that he had personally been asked to perform since the deceased had expressed an admiration for his work. Now he was standing at the graveside and pronouncing the age-old words of comfort for the living, while from a distance came the still unfamiliar sound of the whine of jet engines.

Orville Wright, who was in his seventy-seventh year, had died during the night of Friday 30 January to the surprise of some; a visitor only two years before having described him as 'young-looking, with an alert mind, interested in a wide number of subjects'. He left only the equivalent of £267,000.

The sound of the Air Force jets rose to a climax as the four* swept in formation low over Woodland Cemetery, dipping their wings in respect as they did so. In a moment they were gone, climbing into the February sky, their pilots' faces stern and set, not only from concentration on their task but also from the realisation that they had given a final salute to the last survivor of the two most senior of the men who had changed the world.

Shortly afterwards, on 6 February, His Honor Judge Love of the Probate Court of Dayton, Ohio, announced the contents of a letter dated 8 December 1943, addressed to Colonel E.E.B. Macintosh, then Director of the Science Museum, South Kensington, London, England. In it Orville Wright had stated: 'I have decided to have the Kitty Hawk† returned to America when transport

---

* Five aircraft had been intended originally.

† Reference to the machine as the 'Kitty Hawk' is interesting; previous references to it had been as the 'Wright Flyer', first used in 1908.

hazards are less than at present. I will let you know later the time for its return.' The colonel replied on 15 February 1944, to the effect that he was not surprised at Orville's decision, adding that it was unsafe for the machine to be sent overseas at that time. The reason for the display of the machine in England rather than the United States had been due to an earlier official expression by the Smithsonian Institution of doubts about the Wrights' claim to have been the first men to achieve sustained, controlled flight. However, in 1943 the then curator had formally apologised to Orville for the doubts expressed by his predecessor, Orville accepting this and assuring him that the aircraft would be returned to the USA. Unfortunately, nothing could be done at the time due to the war. The aircraft had been in Great Britain since 1928, having been dispatched, now renovated after a trial assembly, in three packing cases; these were duly placed aboard the SS *Minnewaska* of the Atlantic Transport Line which sailed on 11 February and arrived in England nine days later.

On 25 February the cases were opened at the Science Museum, erection starting on 9 March. The 'Flyer' was placed on exhibition three days later, and was not moved again until the Munich Crisis of September 1938 when concerns

The plane that changed the world. The Wright brothers' 'Flyer' as it appeared when first displayed at the Science Museum, South Kensington, London. It was to remain in England for twenty years until it was finally returned home in 1948, a twelve-strong crew of gallery assistants being required to manhandle it out of the display before carefully taking it apart for dispatch (Bruce Robertson Collection)

arose for the machine's safety in the event of war being declared. Thus, on 28 September it was dismantled and stored in the basement in the original cases, only to be replaced a month later, soon to be protected against bomb blast in case Neville Chamberlain's assurance of 'peace for our time' proved false.

However, early in July 1940 the 'Flyer' was again dismantled and returned to the museum basement until it was removed in April 1942 to the safety of a quarry, 100 feet deep, at Corsham, having been duly treated with preservative. In February 1943 it was moved again, this time to the nearby 70 feet deep Admiralty quarry, also at Corsham, where temperature and humidity control was possible. There it remained until returned to the Science Museum aviation gallery on the evening of 7 June 1945, inspection revealing no damage except slight rusting of some metal parts. It was subsequently returned to exhibition, a report confirming that it was to be seen again at the end of May 1946.

On 18 October 1948, the 'Flyer' was lowered to the museum's floor and prepared for its journey home. It was first dismantled once more and taken by road to Southampton and there loaded aboard the Cunard-White Star Line's SS *Mauretania* which departed for New York on 6 November, arriving six days later; the 'Flyer' was officially handed over to the Smithsonian Institution on 17 December 1948. On 17 December 1945 the Science Museum had announced that it was hoped a replica would be constructed by members of the de Havilland training school for only the cost of materials plus 10 per cent. The offer had been accepted, and the replica delivered in the following September, later replacing the original in the aviation gallery.

With the approach of the centenary of the historic first flight, attention focused anew on the preservation of surviving specimens, so that one of the first of these scheduled for renovation was the Wright Type 'B', reportedly NR 14333, in the Franklin Institute, Philadelphia. This particular machine was of interest not only because it was powered by a 30-hp Wright engine. Purchased for $5,000 (equivalent to some $100,000 today) by eighteen-year-old Grover Cleveland Bergoll in 1912, this is believed to be the fourteenth example constructed. Bergoll regularly flew the aircraft from a field some 7 miles west of Philadelphia, clocking up a total of 300 hours during 748 trips, until it was put into storage in 1914 only to emerge in 1934 on presentation to the institute. Selected for reconditioning by the Aeroplane Works company of New Carlisle, Ohio, in March 2001, the Franklin Institute's senior curator, John Alvinti, claimed, 'It is better than the 1903 "Flyer" at the Smithsonian. It has more original fabric and is in better shape.' The $100,000 necessary for this machine's restoration was met by philanthropists John and Terry Desmond.

THE WRIGHT CONSTRUCTION METHODS

Even apart from the massive implications for every sphere of civilised life wrought by the achievement of powered flight, one hundred years ago it was also instrumental in creating a new type of engineering and thereby, an industry. So it is worth taking a look, however fleeting, at the first showing of this new field of human creative endeavour, recording a few constructional details of the original Wright 'Flyer' and its engine, all the while remembering that Wilbur and Orville were filling a virgin page in human achievement with no precedents to guide them, and that they were not trained engineers, merely very gifted bicycle-makers. If a token of their modest technical background is needed, proof may surely be found in the small detail of the roller to engage the launching rail of their later flying machines – it was the hub of a motorcycle wheel.

THE AIRFRAME

Construction of the 1903 'Flyer' was predominantly of timber, the wings having spruce ribs and tips while ash formed the main spar/leading edges (there was no main spar as such on Wright-designed wings), the latter being 1 inch by 1 inch timber with the entering edge rounded. Ash was also used for the short, central trailing edge which supported the upper, horizontal struts carrying the compound rudder.

The stringy grain and elasticity of spruce made it an obvious choice for the interplane struts however, the timber here being of oval section $1^{15}/_{16}$ inch by $\frac{3}{4}$ inch at the centre tapering to 1 inch by $\frac{3}{4}$ inch at the extremities, each of which carries an eye to engage a metal clip fastened to grip the front or rear spar, each of which in turn formed into a pair of hooks providing anchorage points for the wing bracing. The trailing edge of the wings was of piano wire, this enclosed in a pocket in the 'rubber cloth' fabric covering, which was also fastened to the ribs with the aid of tape. Similar construction was employed for the elevators where

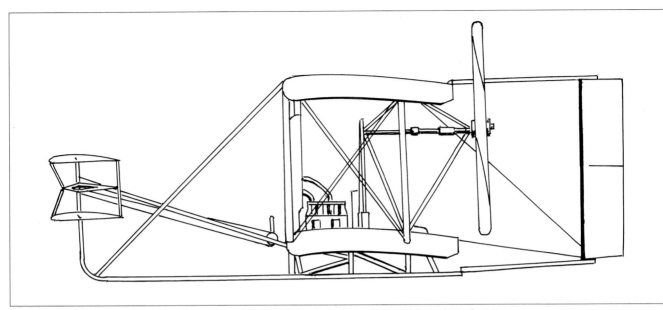

Comparative side elevations of (above) the original Wright 'Flyer' of 1903 and (below) the Wright Type 'A' of 1907/8. *(Author's collection)*

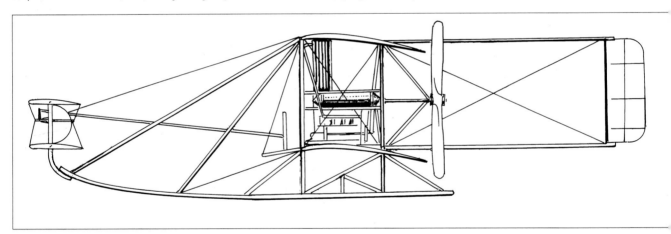

spruce was used throughout with similar muslin covering, while spruce and ash together were employed for the framework of the rudders which were fabric-covered on both sides. There was no fixed vertical surface, the absence of a fin resulting in a machine that had to be continuously controlled.

It is not generally realised that the Wright biplane carried instruments, although these were of a simple nature and minimal in number. These consisted of only three, all mounted on one of the forward centre-section struts within the pilot's field of vision and were an anemometer to register velocity, a revolution counter and a stopwatch.

The original airscrew shafts were tubular but showed a tendency to fracture so that they were replaced by solid shafts. Airscrews were solid spruce, not laminated and had their tips covered with fabric.

British licence-built Wright Type 'A' biplanes were advertised at £1,200 when powered by a 30-hp Léon Bollée or Barriquand & Marre built Wright engine; those powered by a 30-hp Green motor were slightly cheaper, marketed at 'from £1,100'.

Tuition on a customer's own machine was available at £50 and a new machine was guaranteed to be capable of a 20-mile flight with a passenger aboard when flown in a closed circuit.

The original Wright engine seen here upright as it was exhibited in 1928. When used to power the 1903 'Flyer', it was mounted on its side. *(Courtesy of Special Collections and Archives, Wright State University, Ohio)*

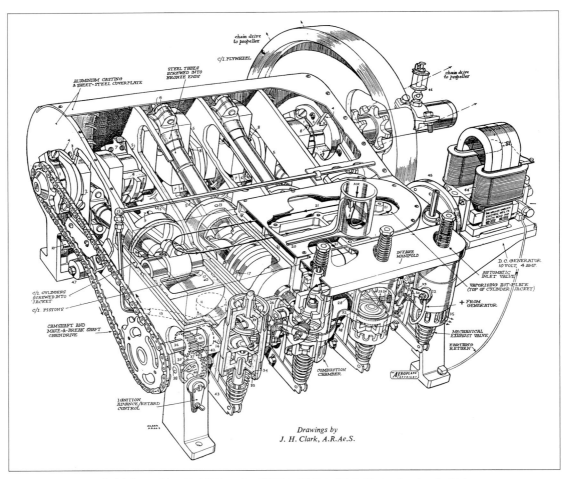

Exploded view of the original Wright engine of 1903 by J.H. Clark, ARAeS. (*Courtesy* Aeroplane Monthly)

KEY

1. and 2.   Bearing caps in one piece with plate 3
3.   Plate screws over hole 4 in crankcase end
4.   Key-shaped hole as hole 5 in intermediate ribs
6.   Inter-bearings cap (white-metal lined) and screwed to inter-rib halves 7
8.   Splash-drip feed to bearings
9.   Return to pump from each compartment of crankcase base ('sump') via gallery 10 and pipe to pump 11 underneath jacket
12.   Oil feed from pump via rubber tube 13
13.   Drip feeds to cylinders and pistons
14.   Gear drive to pump
15.   Big-end nuts, lock-strip and shims
16.   Gudgeon-pin lock
17.   Piston-ring retainer pegs
18.   Cylinder liner screwed into jacket
19.   Open-ended 'can' admits air
20.   Fuel supply

21.   (Hot) side of water-jacket makes surface carburettor
22.   Sparking plug (comprising positive electrode 23 and spark producing make-and-break 24)
25.   Lever attached to lever 26 via bearing 27 screwed into neck 28
26.   Levers with mainspring 29 and interspring 30, and rocked by 'cam' 31
31.   Cam with another alongside (for adjacent cylinder)
32.   Positive busbar feed to all four cylinders
33.   Assembly retaining-rings
34.   Sealing disc
35.   Exhaust outlet ports
36.   Camshaft right along on underside of jacket and also driving oil pump 11 via 14
37.   Spring-loaded sliding pinion drives make-and-break shaft 38 through peg in inclined slot 39
40.   Cam to push pinion 37 along and so alter its angular relation with shaft 38 (to vary timing)
41.   Exhaust-valve cams bear on rollers 42 mounted in end of rocker arms 43
44.   Generator floating coils
45.   Friction-drive off flywheel
46.   Sight-feed lubricator (on stationary sleeve)
47.   Hardwood chain tensioner

THE MOTOR

Agreement on the weight of the machine is not unanimous, 170 lb, 180 lb and 240 lb all being quoted at various times and by various authorities, some without making clear whether the flywheel and magneto were included. However, 152 lb is now regarded as a reliable figure, other numerical data being bore, 4 inches, stroke, 4 inches, while the take-off rpm of 1,020 gave 12 hp.

Those who have heard a replica engine of this type at full throttle will have been surprised by the comparatively low noise level, although on the actual aircraft this must have been higher, largely due to the noise that must have been created by the airscrew-drive chains running in their tubular guide-tubes.

As a piece of engineering, the Wright motor is certainly simple, yet this flat, four-cylinder, in-line water-cooled motor that ran on its side was ingenious in several particulars, the main one for some being the manner in which the pistons and big ends were lubricated by a drip-feed arrangement. Moreover, comment is nearly always excited by discussion of the way in which the camshaft chain is tensioned by means, not of a metal pulley, but one of hardwood!

But perhaps the most novel feature of the original Wright motor was the ignition system which fired petrol vapour from a small cylindrical chamber into which it had been led before heating and therefore vapourising by the heat created by the normal running of the engine. This was ignited by a special system whereby a secondary shaft fitted with sheet metal cams, in revolving pressed spring-loaded levers against a series of stops; as the cams slipped off the ends of these levers, a spark was created and the petrol vapour in the related cylinder head fired. A wide copper strip bolted to the outsides of the individual cylinders provided a common lead and completed the electrical circuit of this simple make-and-break system.

Like the aeroplane it powered, the ingenious engineering of this little motor is astonishing, designed as it was by a pair of self-effacing bicycle-makers who had chosen for their experiments one hundred years ago, a wild spot on the Carolina seaboard that had scarcely seen mankind since 1587, when Raleigh's colonists had attempted to settle a short distance further south on Roanoke Island. How astonished Orville must have been to learn, less than thirty years after he and his brother had first taken to the air from that spot before going home for Christmas, that fashionable tourists were actually flying into the little nearby airstrip. Small wonder that a crisply worded advertisement could confidently announce: 'Flying no longer requires preface or apology.'

The autumn of 1901 had seen the Wrights working on their third glider, based on the experience and disappointments of No. 2, while a motor was as yet undreamt of. By coincidence almost a century later engineers in Britain and France would be toiling to restore Concorde to its former proud position after the tragic events of 26 July 2000, when one of the fleet crashed shortly after take-off just outside Paris. Now in a sense, the success of the Wright brothers was bearing fruit anew in a design capable of outpacing the very speed of sound, driven by some 38,000 lb of thrust; a power unimaginable when a tiny 12-hp petrol motor drove the world's first flying machine for 58 seconds over a distance of 850 feet.

AFTERWORD

The tall figure that emerged from the shed with an air of modest self-assurance, pulling on his coat, was immediately identifiable as Wilbur Wright; he quickened his stride to meet the Englishman he knew had been waiting for him for some time and whom he now greeted with an unexpected salutation: 'Now Mr Brewer, we'll go and have some dinner.' It was a strange welcome and one that was to have far-reaching consequences for the future of European flying; words uttered late one August day in 1908, far from the homes of both men in a field at Le Mans, France.

The Englishman whom Wilbur addressed was the wealthy patents agent Griffith Brewer, currently trading from 33 Chancery Lane, London. Born forty-one years before at Devereux Court, off Fleet Street, in his spare time he had managed to rekindle enthusiasm for the Edwardian sport of ballooning, having made his first ascent with Auguste Caudron in 1891. He went on to participate as the pilot of balloons entered in the Gordon Bennett races of 1906, 1907, 1908 and later 1922, the first three beginning respectively from Paris, St Louis and Berlin. Additionally, in 1908 he took part in the Hurlingham International Balloon Race, accompanied by Sir Claude Champion de Crespigny, an event in which Brewer's vessel beat no less than thirty other competitors. Griffith later experimented with a series of small balloons intended to act as photographic platforms; from these were taken some of the very first aerial views of London.

Over the simple dinner which they shared on the evening of their first meeting, the two men soon realised that they had much in common and a friendship quickly sprang up; in a sense this was confirmed when, on 8 October, Wilbur offered to take Brewer, the confirmed lighter-than-air enthusiast, up for a flight in a heavier-than-air craft. Griffith accepted, so becoming the first Englishman to make an aeroplane flight – albeit as a passenger. On the same day, among those given subsequent trips from Camp d'Auvours were the Hon. C.S. Rolls, another balloonist and destined to become the first man to fly the English Channel in both directions non-stop; Frank

Hedges Butler, co-founder of the Aero Club of Great Britain, in 1901; and Major B.F.S. Baden-Powell, brother of the creator of the Boy Scout Movement and responsible for assisting with the development of British military ballooning, also acting secretary of the Aeronautical Society.

The friendship of Wilbur Wright and Griffith Brewer continued to deepen after the latter's meeting with Orville. After a second trip to France during the next year and following fresh demonstrations by Wilbur at Pau, Brewer enthusiastically cabled Eustace Short, currently constructing balloons beneath the Battersea railway arches near the site of today's Dogs' Home. Eustace at once dispatched his brother Horace to France where he was able to make drawings of Wright machines, subsequently manufacturing six, thus aiding the firm's changeover to the construction of aeroplanes, something which it had attempted earlier but without success. Griffith Brewer now having clearly demonstrated his ability as a publicist, it was not long before he was offered the job of European sales manager by the Wrights, work that Wilbur had attempted to undertake in May 1907, making a special trip to Europe in order to publicise the Wright Flyer III in London, Paris, Moscow and Berlin.

Brewer accepted the brothers' offer; sadly, one of his first duties was to undertake the foundation of the British Wright Company after Wilbur's death in 1912, arranging that the new organisation take over the Wright patents in England, becoming recognised himself as an authority on aircraft patents in the process. At the same time he inaugurated the annual Wilbur Wright Memorial Lecture in memory of his friend, reading the fourth of these papers himself and also acting as the honorary secretary of the memorial.

In 1914, Griffith travelled to the United States where he gained pilot's licence No. 9245 at the Wright school, Dayton, Ohio just after the outbreak of the First World War. During the conflict he was appointed Honorary Adviser to the Roehampton Kite Balloon School, at the same time carrying out a large number of experiments involving kite balloons and training several hundred airship and kite balloon officers and men.

Griffith Brewer was to die at his Walton-on-Thames home on 1 March 1946, having obtained an autogiro pilot's licence in 1933 and having flown his personal light aircraft regularly and safely until he was well advanced in age. He served for many years on the council of the Royal Aeronautical Society, acting as its vice-president for a lengthy period and as president from 1940 to 1942, continuing to attend meetings of the society until shortly before his death. One youthful attendant remembered him as having a benign disposition in old age, looking towards the future of aviation with confidence, believing that it would be secure in the hands of the young, as it had been in his own time. For Brewer those were the golden years, now little chronicled and scarcely remembered, when he had grappled on behalf of the Wrights against the rather dubious claims in favour of the Langley machine. A lengthy struggle which was eventually triumphant, vindicating the claims of the brothers from Dayton.

And tomorrow? *(British Airways)*

BIBLIOGRAPHY

Bowen, E., *Knights of the Air*. Time-Life Books, 1980

Boyne, W.J., *Smithsonian Book of Flight*. Sidgwick & Jackson, 1987

Brewer, G., *Fifty Years of Flying*. Air League, 1946

Bruce, Gordon, *Charlie Rolls*. Rolls-Royce Heritage Trust, 1990

Bruce, J.M., *Aircraft of the Royal Flying Corps*. Putnam, 1982

Clarke, D., *Aircraft and Airports*. Arco Publishing, 1978

Crouch, T.D., *The Bishop's Boys*. W.W. Norton, 1989

Dale, H., *Early Flying Machines*. British Library, 1992

Edwards C., *Golden Jubilee of Flying*. Associated Newspapers, 1953

Fabb, J., *Flying and Ballooning*. Batsford, 1980

Gibbs-Smith, C.H., *Early Flying Machines*. Eyre Methuen, 1975

——, *Pioneers of the Aeroplane*. Usborne, 1975

——, *The Wright Brothers*. H.M.S.O., 1986

Harper, H., *My Fifty Years in Flying*. Associated Newspapers, 1956

Harrison, M., *Airborne at Kitty Hawk*. Cassell, 1953

Howard, F., *Wilbur and Orville*. Robert Hale, 1987

Jackson, R., *Guinness Book of Air Warfare*. Guinness, 1993

Kelly, F.C., *The Wright Brothers*. Harrap, 1956

King, P., *Knights of the Air*. Constable, 1989

Lewis, P., *British Aircraft 1809–1914*. Putnam, 1962

Longyard, W.H., *Who's Who in Aviation History*. Airlife, 1994

Lopez, D.S., *Aviation*. Macmillan Smithsonian Guide Series, 1995

Reynolds, Q., *They Fought for the Sky*. Cassell, 1956

Spick, M., *Milestones of Manned Flight*. Salamander, 1994

Swanborough, F.G., *United States Military Aircraft since 1909*. Putnam, 1963

——, *United States Naval Aircraft since 1911*. Putnam, 1968

Taylor, J.W.R., *A Pictorial History of Flight*. Hulton Press, 1955

Taylor, M., *Guinness Book of Aircraft Facts and Feats*. Guinness, 1984

Westcott, L., *Wind and Sand*. Harry N. Abrams, 1983

NEWSPAPERS
Daily Mail
Gulf Today
Le Petit Journal
New York Herald Tribune
The Times

MAGAZINES
Aeromodeller
Aeroplane
Cross and Cockade Society Journal
Flight International (formerly *Flight*)
Flying
Icare
National Geographic magazine
Royal Aero Club Gazette
Royal Aeronautical Society magazine
Royal Aeronautical Society Garden Party Programme 1957

INDEX